Evidencing Teaching Achievements
in Higher Education

CRITICAL PRACTICE IN HIGHER EDUCATION

Acknowledgements

We wish to thank our former colleagues from Newcastle University, who were involved in establishing and maintaining a strategic project to reward and recognise teaching: in particular, Suzanne Cholerton, Ellie Clewlow, Richard Harrison and Claire Irving. Thanks are due to Steve's colleagues on the Higher Education Academy Promoting Teaching project, the late Annette Cashmore and Sandra Wills, along with the other team members Chris Cane, Christine Brown, David Sadler and especially Sue Robson. Thanks too to other colleagues with whom we have had the privilege of exploring the challenge of evidencing teaching achievements over the years, in the contexts of universities, the Staff and Educational Development Association (SEDA) and Advance HE.

We would like to thank the Series Editors Joy Jarvis and Karen Mpamhanga, who have provided unflagging support, insight and encouragement as well as editorial support.

Finally, this book has been long in its gestation so thanks must go to our families who have had to tolerate our absences while we wrote and revised the text. Steve's partner, Jackie, could not have expected that even after their retirements he would still be spending quite so much time at his desk. Steve would say how grateful he is to Jackie for her patience, forbearance and support throughout this time. Marita would like to acknowledge the unfailing support of her family: deepest thanks to Jonathan, to Jacob and to Theo.

To order our books please go to our website www.criticalpublishing.com or contact our distributor Ingram Publisher Services, telephone 01752 202301 or email IPSUK. orders@ingramcontent.com. Details of bulk order discounts can be found at www.criticalpublishing.com/delivery-information.

Our titles are also available in electronic format: for individual use via our website and for libraries and other institutions from all the major ebook platforms.

Evidencing Teaching Achievements
in Higher Education

Marita Grimwood and Steve McHanwell

Series Editors: Joy Jarvis and Karen Mpamhanga

CRITICAL PRACTICE IN HIGHER EDUCATION

First published in 2024 by Critical Publishing Ltd

All rights reserved. No part of this publication may be reproduced, stored in a retrieval system, or transmitted in any form or by any means, electronic, mechanical, photocopying, recording or otherwise, without prior permission in writing from the publisher.

The authors have made every effort to ensure the accuracy of information contained in this publication, but assume no responsibility for any errors, inaccuracies, inconsistencies and omissions. Likewise, every effort has been made to contact copyright holders. If any copyright material has been reproduced unwittingly and without permission the Publisher will gladly receive information enabling them to rectify any error or omission in subsequent editions.

Copyright © 2024 Marita Grimwood and Steve McHanwell

British Library Cataloguing in Publication Data
A CIP record for this book is available from the British Library

ISBN: 978-1-915080-6-22

This book is also available in the following e-book formats:
EPUB ISBN: 978-1-915080-6-39
Adobe e-book ISBN: 978-1-915080-6-46

The rights of Marita Grimwood and Steve McHanwell to be identified as the Authors of this work have been asserted by them in accordance with the Copyright, Design and Patents Act 1988.

Text and cover design by Out of House Limited
Project Management by Newgen Publishing UK

Critical Publishing
3 Connaught Road
St Albans
AL3 5RX
www.criticalpublishing.com

Contents

	Meet the authors and series editors	*vi*
	Book summary	*viii*
Chapter 1	Teaching and learning in contemporary higher education	1
Chapter 2	Defining teaching quality in higher education	10
Chapter 3	Building an education-focused career	25
Chapter 4	Evidencing the effectiveness of teaching	40
Chapter 5	Presenting the evidence	58
Chapter 6	Support for applicants	74
Chapter 7	Institutional perspectives on teaching evidence and some conclusions	88
	References	*101*
	Index	*107*

Meet the authors and series editors

Marita Grimwood is an Educational Developer whose career has spanned academic, professional and freelance roles. Marita has particular interests in internationalised, inclusive curricula; and in evidencing and recognising learning, teaching and its leadership in higher education. She has led and contributed to projects on these and other topics institutionally, nationally, and internationally, and given numerous invited workshops. She is an experienced designer, leader and external examiner of professional development programmes, and previously led the Staff and Educational Development Association's (SEDA) Fellowships scheme. Initially teaching and publishing in English Literature, in which she holds a PhD, her current research and scholarship focuses on learning and teaching. A Principal Fellow of the Higher Education Academy and Fellow of SEDA, she is currently a Senior Adviser in Teaching Fellowships at Advance HE, leading on Principal Fellowship.

Steve McHanwell is Emeritus Professor of Anatomical Sciences at Newcastle University and a National Teaching Fellow. He is currently employed part time at the University of Edinburgh. He has had a long-standing interest in parity of esteem and evidencing of teaching, having led two working parties in 2011–13 and again in 2017–20, making a series of recommendations leading to significant policy changes in this area in Newcastle. He was co-project lead for Newcastle in the Higher Education Academy Promoting Teaching project. He has led workshops in this area in Newcastle and is a frequent speaker and workshop leader for other universities.

MEET THE AUTHORS AND SERIES EDITORS

Joy Jarvis is Professor of Educational Practice at the University of Hertfordshire and a UK National Teaching Fellow. She has experience in a wide range of education contexts and works to create effective learning experiences for students and colleagues. She is particularly interested in the professional learning of those engaged in educational practice in higher education settings and has undertaken a range of projects, working with colleagues locally, nationally and internationally, to develop practice in teaching and leadership of teaching. Joy works with doctoral students exploring aspects of educational practice and encourages them to be adventurous in their methodological approaches and to share their findings to enable practice change.

Karen Mpamhanga (formerly Karen Smith) is Professor of Higher Education and Professional Learning in the Schools of Law and Education at the University of Hertfordshire. Her research focuses on how higher education policies and practices impact on those who work and study within universities. Karen has worked within educational development and on lecturer development programmes. She holds a Principal Fellowship of the Higher Education Academy. Karen contributes to the University's Professional Doctorate in Education as a supervisor and cohort leader. She also leads collaborative research and development in her School, where she engages in externally funded research and evaluation and supports the development of scholarly educational practice.

Book summary

This book explores the background and the context in which evidence for effective teaching needs to be provided. It explains the sources and forms of evidence that might be sought for teaching achievements, and how they can be triangulated. The book analyses and evaluates the different forms of evidence available, and how individuals can use evidence to develop a narrative of teaching impact. It provides a framework by which institutions might seek to support staff in collecting and critically deploying evidence of achievements in a range of contexts – whether those staff are on teaching-focused tracks or have teaching as part of a mixed research/teaching portfolio. This book is of value to individuals looking to evidence teaching achievements and to institutions wishing to support and reward academic and professional staff who undertake teaching as part of their professional roles.

Chapter 1 | Teaching and learning in contemporary higher education

Introduction

Finding ways to evidence the effectiveness of teaching is crucial for both individual educators and higher education institutions if they are to identify and meet students' educational needs. In the context of the primacy of metrics in measurements of university performance in teaching and research and the contested nature as to what constitutes teaching excellence (Bamber, 2020), thinking about what evidence of effective learning and teaching looks like is important because institutions need to have their own internal debates to challenge, explore and better appreciate what is genuinely impactful. Individual teachers need to critically engage with the evidence of their own teaching impacts and, in the face of such evidence, be supported to take risks with their pedagogical approaches to explore and develop effective and inspiring ways of supporting their students to learn. A lack of criticality and a reluctance to be exploratory threatens to undermine student learning and the university's role in education. This is not the last word on this issue, and learning and teaching communities in and across the sector need to take ownership of it in different contexts. When and why do we need to evidence teaching achievements? The contexts for it vary and include individual promotion; applying for different forms of professional accreditation and recognition; individual and group teaching awards; and institutional quality assurance management.

'Teaching' is the word often used when describing the education functions that higher education institutions undertake but it is a deceptive term in this context. Using the word teaching evokes activities that take place with students in lecture theatres, seminar rooms, laboratories, clinics and in a range of synchronous and asynchronous formats online. In higher education what is often simply referred to as teaching covers a huge range of educational activity. University teachers are expected not simply to be effective in their interactions with their students in their classrooms – in face-to-face, online or hybrid formats – and as supervisors of undergraduate or postgraduate research, but to engage in a broad range of additional activity. This includes maintaining currency in their discipline either as scholars or as researchers. It may also include management and design of programmes, pastoral care of students and educational leadership. It can also encompass contributing to the scholarship of teaching and learning (SoTL) in their discipline. We will return to the complexity of the educational function in later chapters but why is it, among all this complexity and the activity that it generates, necessary to evidence the impacts of those educational activities and what justification is there for a book on evidencing teaching? There are three possible answers to this question.

The first answer lies in the increasing marketisation of higher education that has taken place in recent decades. The second answer lies in the tensions that exist between teaching and research in many institutions. Finally, while both answers have contributed to the drive towards better approaches to evidencing teaching effectiveness, there is a more important answer that subsumes both. It is our firm belief that there are intrinsic benefits to teaching that flow from the rigorous discussion of the evidence of the effectiveness of teaching. It is only by engaging critically with that evidence that we can understand how our students perceive our teaching. Looking through our students' eyes at the teaching they receive from us is one important part of helping our students to learn (Brookfield, 2017).

The development of a competitive market for students in higher education both nationally and internationally is a continuing trend. Higher education is an expensive activity and governments, whether in relation to their own countries or funding their own students to study abroad, need to feel assured that the money they are investing in education is being well spent. Students who are spending their own money or that of their families require similar assurance. The response to this has been an increasing emphasis on the quality assurance of teaching in universities.

Though education remains a key activity for most universities and constitutes the source of the majority of their income, in many universities educational activity continues to struggle for parity of esteem with research. We outline some of the historical background to this both below in this chapter and later in this book, but in essence research remains a key determinant of the prestige of an institution. Partly because of this prestige element and partly because much evidence of research impact resides in external data and is often metrics-driven, there is a perception – often a correct one – that greater reward and recognition is given to high-profile research staff. By way of contrast, evidencing excellence in teaching is felt by many to be difficult and contested. This is partly because much of that evidence resides within the institution and may be sensitive or raise issues of confidentiality. It also raises issues of interpretation because it involves mixed-methods approaches, blending qualitative with quantitative data. Developing better shared understandings of what constitutes rigour in evidencing of teaching is one part of the answer to this problem. This book is designed to help individuals, teams and institutions to do this.

Quality in higher education

The emergence of a discourse of teaching excellence in higher education came about against the backdrop of a dominant discourse of research excellence: the use of measures of research performance to determine research quality and then the aggregation of those measures to produce ranking tables of university performance internationally.

University ranking tables have a longer history than is sometimes realised. The first ones emerged in the 1920s in the US and were produced to allow comparison of research performance in US universities. Since the 1980s the globalisation of universities, combined with a neoliberal drive to create a marketplace for national and international student recruitment, has stimulated a desire among universities to seek markers of prestige that enable students to differentiate them from their competitors. The compiling of ranking tables has greatly expanded consequently to fulfil this need for prestige markers.

Universities are one major source of knowledge development, turning money into knowledge, which can perhaps then be turned back into money. In knowledge economies, knowledge is an important source of not just economic but also social and political power. Therefore, tables which rank universities to show which countries have often invested large amounts of money can be viewed by those countries as proxy measures for societal economic progress (Brink, 2018). The perceived authority of those tables is increased because they are compiled by external sources rather than the universities or countries themselves and so acquire a semblance of objectivity and transparency.

Such tables are not without considerable difficulties, however (Brink, 2018). One of these difficulties emerges from the prestige effects they create (Blackmore, 2016). Obviously, only one university can be top of a table, in the top five, or in the top 200 club seen as important by many countries when seeking to fund students to study in universities internationally. Ranking tables claim to challenge preconceived notions of superiority, though in reality university rankings are fairly stable with relatively little movement among the highly ranked institutions. Another difficulty is that the assumption made by the compilers of these tables is that universities are all rather similar in their missions. Often this is not the case because missions and strengths of universities vary, and ranking tables can obscure the fact that they may not be comparing like for like (Brink, 2018). There is a risk, therefore, that one unintended effect of ranking tables is to force universities seeking high rankings into a degree of conformity, with universities seeking to adjust the missions or submissions of data to the demands, as it were, of the test. In response to these two difficulties, there has been a proliferation of tables that rank universities regionally or tables that rank universities on different criteria, for example, sustainability. A key international player in the production of ranking tables is Times Higher Education. Other international ranking tables produced include the QS World University Rankings and the Academic Ranking of World Universities (ARWU). Several countries also produce national ranking tables. In the UK, for example, tables are produced by three national newspapers: *The Guardian*, *The Times* and *The Sunday Times*. *The Guardian*, for example, uses data on full-time first-degree courses using data provided on university courses by the Office for Students. It uses eight criteria (entry levels, expenditure/student, continuation, overall student satisfaction, student satisfaction with feedback, value-added and career prospects) to produce individual subject ranking tables which are then used to compile overall university ranking tables.

Example 1.1

Sample ranking table

An example of the way in which international ranking tables are produced is given by QS World University Rankings, who publish annually their ranking criteria and the weighting they attach to each criterion (QS World University Rankings, 2023). In this example the published criteria for 2024 are provided. To be included in the ranking table universities must also fulfil the eligibility criteria of QS World University Rankings.

Table 1.1 2024 criteria, with weightings, for QS World University Rankings

Performances lenses	2024 edition weights	Change from previous editions
Academic reputation	30%	10% deducted
Employer reputation	15%	5% added
Faculty student ratio	10%	10% deducted
Citations per faculty	20%	No change
International faculty ratio	5%	No change
International student ratio	5%	No change
International research network	5%	New
Employment outcomes	5%	New

QS World University Rankings publish a series of tables alongside QS World University Ranking tables and QS World University Rankings by subject. Tables produced include separate university rankings for Europe, Asia, Latin America and the Caribbean and Arab regions. They also produce QS Sustainability Rankings and ranking for Global MBA and Business Masters.

The position of a university or subject will obviously be determined by its score for each criterion but also by the weighting attached to each criterion. Brink (2018) shows in a detailed analysis how small changes in weightings can produce quite marked effects on the positions of universities in league tables. As he points out, this is a feature of all such ranking tables, meaning that caution is necessary when viewing the results.

These difficulties are not least an issue when it comes to matters of presumed teaching excellence. Ranking tables can have an inbuilt tendency to over-emphasise research performance. This may not be so much a case of bias but rather the availability of data and its contested value (Gunn and Fisk, 2013; Gourlay and Stephenson, 2017; Wood and Su, 2017). Research performance data is much more visible in the public domain. Measures such as research funding, publications or citations are available from external sources and represent more direct measures of research performance – albeit subject to debate in some cases, such as citations. They are key drivers of academic reputation, as shown in Example 1.1.

Data on teaching excellence is generated internally and tables such as that in Example 1.1 rely largely on proxy measures such as entry requirements for students, proportions of students gaining good degrees, student satisfaction data, staff–student ratios and student destination data. None of these measures can be said to represent in any satisfactory way teaching excellence (a contested concept anyway, as it is experienced in the classroom in terms of its effectiveness and impact upon the quality of student learning [see Chapter 2]). On this basis universities may seek to frame quality of their teaching as excellent or world leading in the same way as similar claims are made for research performance, though ultimately it is not clear what that means. One formulation which is sometimes put forward is teaching worthy of emulation, though this is hardly amenable to measurement as such.

Another reason for the tendency of teaching rankings to follow research rankings is in situations where academic reputation forms an element of the weighting of the ranking, such as occurs in the table produced by QS World Rankings (see Example 1.1). It is recognised that academic staff asked to rate the reputation of universities in their own academic discipline will often assume that a good research reputation signifies a good teaching reputation as well.

So, can teaching quality be measured and teaching excellence defined? The proxy measures listed above all have intrinsic difficulties in their interpretation. There is an over-reliance on student satisfaction data, but student satisfaction does not, in any straightforward way, equate to good student learning outcomes. A further source of bias may originate from the students when making responses to national surveys of opinion such as the National Student Survey (NSS) in the UK. Students, especially in 'elite' institutions, may avoid giving ratings that would reduce that elite status either from bias or simply because it would partly be an admission of having made a poor choice in deciding which university to go to. Some of the other measures that have been used include the proportion of good degrees a university awards or its ratios of staff to students. The validity of both measures has been challenged: using the proportion of good degrees awarded can encourage grade inflation, while the apparent ratio of staff to students can be inflated by the inclusion of categories of staff who may be only peripherally involved in teaching. We will explore the contested nature of teaching excellence more fully in Chapter 2.

Finally, and as noted above, the perceptions of what a university is trying to achieve in its teaching will play into its narrative of what it views as excellence. Gunn and Fisk (2013), in their review of what constitutes teaching excellence, identify that university teaching missions will often reflect a delicate balance between discipline-specific teaching and teaching to enable entry to a specific profession, alongside teaching discipline-specific skills and more generic transferable skills. The precise balance struck will depend upon the subject mix and student destinations.

Parity of esteem between teaching and research

Although many universities have recognised the importance of acknowledging, and rewarding through promotion, achievements in teaching, in many cases the gap in parity of esteem between teaching and research so evident in the past is still with us today. The issues around the evidencing of teaching effectiveness have been outlined above, but at the heart of the problem is a paradox that arises from the importance of research success as a prestige factor and proxy for the success of a university overall. This is because of the multifaceted nature of the relationship between teaching and research in universities.

In many universities, the income generated by teaching, derived in part from the fees that students pay, is needed to cross-subsidise research. To justify this cross-subsidy, universities have sought to underline the benefits to teaching of having an active research culture. This is achieved through the promotion of teaching that is research linked, an umbrella term meaning the ways in which students may encounter research content and activity during their course. This could be through research-led teaching, where course content is underpinned by current research in a discipline or disciplines. It can also involve research-based teaching, consisting of either small or extended projects that introduce students to enquiry methods in the discipline. The benefits of these approaches are identified as a combination of being taught by academics leading in their respective fields and students being able to undertake research projects.

The expectation is, therefore, that teaching in universities will be delivered by the majority of higher education teachers whatever the nature of their contracts, whether education focused, research focused or one which combines education with research and/or other activities. The involvement in teaching of staff with research and education contracts may involve supervision of undergraduate or postgraduate research, or it may extend to participation in other aspects of undergraduate and postgraduate teaching. For this to work, recognition of the teaching undertaken by staff on a combined research/education contract, even if this represents only a small part of their work, is just as important as it is for education-focused staff. This means that such staff require at least some understanding of how to evidence teaching and other education achievements. They will present that evidence during formalised peer-review career discussions, alongside research achievements such as publication and funding awards, as part of a wider career path that includes research. This extends to early career staff primarily engaged in research, such as research associates who are engaged in some education.

Why is evidencing the impact of teaching important?

Why, in this complex context, do we need to think about evidencing the impact of our educational work? Firstly, the marketisation of higher education, including the introduction of fees in the UK context, has led to a stronger culture of measurement. Secondly, evidencing of teaching is the foundation of serious discussion about tracking an evolving, developing understanding of its evaluation in a way that is embedded, formalised and professionalised and researched through peer-review processes. These processes necessarily differ from those in research where indicators such as peer-reviewed publications, successful external funding applications for research and research impact strongly feature, as in, for example, the UK Research Excellence Framework (REF). However, they need to be of equivalent rigour. In this way, if recognised as such, they can act as a counterbalance of the dominance of research as a prestige indicator in universities (Macfarlane 2007; Blackmore, 2016).

Chapter 2 expands on the discussion started in this chapter by examining in more detail what is meant by teaching excellence, looking at some of the contested conceptions of excellence and its relationship to expert teaching. Following on from this, Chapter 3 examines the diverse and varied nature of teaching careers and the routes to building a career that is education focused, whether as an academic or as a member of professional service staff. Chapter 4 then examines how achievements in educational work might be evidenced during the course of a teaching career. The focus of Chapter 5 is on how the evidence gathered about such achievements can be deployed in developing applications for advancement, including through promotion, awards and other forms of professional accreditation and recognition. Chapter 6 discusses the role of mentors in building an education-focused career and the benefits that mentoring can bring to such a career. Finally, Chapter 7 explores the implications for institutions wishing to support the development of education-focused staff in terms of parity of esteem between education and other functions of a university. How can institutions support an agenda that values education as being of equivalent status to the other functions of a university, including research?

A note on case studies: one of the premises of this book is that 'teaching' in higher education refers to a wide range of education-focused activity. To further illustrate some of the issues we explore in this book, we have included five career case studies of individual staff. We sought initial permission for these via a combination of personal approaches and requests on mailing lists, and the final versions have also been approved for publication by the individuals. They have also all agreed to their inclusion without anonymisation. To create the case studies, we drew on promotion and/or teaching award applications, as appropriate, to highlight the key activities which contributed to achieving these.

Critical questions for practice

Reflecting on career development

- » How would you describe the current balance between teaching and research in your own career?
- » What are the contexts as you understand them for rewarding and recognising teaching in your own institution?
- » What do you see as your responses to developing your career in the light of your answers to the first two questions?
- » On what is your understanding based?

Summary

- The term teaching is often used to describe activities related to working directly with students. However, learning and teaching work in higher education also encompasses different kinds of leadership, scholarship and the development of resources and learning environments (online, face to face and hybrid), alongside pastoral and academic support of students.
- How higher education teaching is understood is closely tied to its perceived relationship with research, which is highly variable and contextual.
- Evidencing achievements in teaching serves a huge number of practical purposes in the context of contemporary higher education. These range from those relating to the individual learner to those concerned with institutional quality management.
- If we are to communicate the value of teaching, both internally and to prospective students, or to challenge and influence national policies, as a sector we must find ways to evidence and disseminate the impact of our teaching in ways in which we feel confident.

Useful texts

Blackmore, P (2016) *Prestige in Academic Life: Excellence and Exclusion*. New York: Routledge.

A detailed analysis of the central role that prestige plays in discourses surrounding ideas of university excellence and the dominant role that research plays in that discourse.

Brink, C (2018) *The Soul of a University*. Bristol: Bristol University Press.

An extended discussion of what is understood by quality in a university, the role that the rise of ranking tables has played in that discussion and what can be understood when we use the term 'a good university'.

Lea, J (ed) (2015) *Enhancing Learning and Teaching in Higher Education: Engaging with the Dimensions of Practice*. Maidenhead: McGraw Hill Education, Open University Press.

A wide-ranging book that touches upon many of the issues raised in the present work. Chapters 7 and 8 are particularly relevant to the issues raised in this chapter.

Chapter 2 | Defining teaching quality in higher education

Nothing that a university does is more important than its teaching.

Baroness Tessa Blackstone, former Labour Minister of Education
and Provost of Birkbeck College, London

In this perfectly weighted statement, what is Baroness Blackstone trying to tell us? What she is not saying is that teaching is the most important thing that a university does. Rather, she is saying that nothing, including research, is more important than the teaching a university provides for its undergraduate and postgraduate students. It is a statement with the clear implication that where a university is carrying out a multiplicity of functions, there should be parity of esteem between those functions, including between teaching and research as outlined in Chapter 1. Yet research has come to dominate as a measure of university prestige, determining positions in world ranking tables and influencing student recruitment, especially in a global market (Blackmore, 2016; Brink, 2018 and see Chapter 1). The response to this dominance of a discourse of research excellence has been the emergence of a discourse of excellence in teaching in an attempt to rebalance the narrative. We are not attempting a full overview of this literature which has been extensively reviewed elsewhere (Gunn and Fisk, 2013; French and O'Leary, 2017; Gourlay and Stephenson, 2017; Tomlinson et al, 2020; Gunn 2023; Chan and Chen, 2023). Here we summarise how key concepts of excellence have come to dominate the teaching landscape and why discourses of teaching excellence can come to undermine teaching. This chapter provides a background to show why evidencing of teaching in critical and nuanced ways, as outlined in Chapters 3 and 4, have come to be so important and how such evidencing might help to underpin a narrative of expertise, expertness and effectiveness (King, 2022).

Gunn and Fisk (2013) identify two discourses in the literature of teaching excellence. The first occurs at an institutional level where measurement of performance by individuals, programmes and units is actively measured and managed through performance indicators. The second occurs at the level of the staff who undertake the teaching and relates to individual performance excellence, driven in part by an agenda of parity of esteem between teaching and research through a reward and recognition agenda.

In Chapter 1, we situated the discourse surrounding teaching quality at the institutional level in higher education, within the broader quality debate surrounding higher education and the performativity agenda. In this chapter, we discuss the highly contested concepts as to what constitutes teaching excellence for individuals, teaching teams and institutions.

Individual teaching performance

Institutional teaching quality judgements in effect result from the aggregation of data from multiple sources. This starts with the work of individual teachers working in large lecture rooms and practical classes, with small groups and with individual students. Data from individuals is progressively aggregated together in schools and faculties, and it is combined with data from professional services supporting learning and teaching and with data about students and learning resources. It makes sense, therefore, to start by looking at teaching quality and teaching excellence through the lens of the contributions made by the staff who teach the students.

That teaching excellence remains a highly contested concept is partly because, as Greatbatch and Holland (2016) observe, excellent teaching involves micro-processes taking place between teachers' individual teaching strategies and students' characteristics as learners. As such it is highly context specific. Excellent teaching is also dependent upon the systems and resources a university has for supporting learning.

As Gunn and Fisk (2013) discuss, part of the problem here lies with the fact that a taxonomy that distinguishes excellent teaching from a threshold standard of teaching that is of good quality has not been articulated. Consequently, there is no consistent approach to how responsibilities and expertise might change over the period of a career and how enhancement and innovation might be judged to be outstanding or be felt to have had impact. Instead, there is a fragmented approach where individual universities draw up such taxonomies to guide decisions about promotion or advancement, or individual teaching award schemes, and devise their own criteria. With that being said, there is a degree of convergence across the sector when it comes to criteria for promotion or advancement in relation to teaching, as seen in published promotion criteria. Despite this, the rhetoric may not always match the reality in the eyes of staff (Cashmore and Ramsden, 2009a, 2009b). Though excellence remains a contested concept there have been attempts to draw up criteria that define good teaching or effective pedagogies. When such attempts are compared, then it is often possible to discern convergence as to what is deemed to constitute 'good' or 'great' teaching.

Reviewing a small group of these attempts to define good teaching using different methodologies, it is possible to arrive at something approaching a consensus. Approaches based upon reviews of research findings (Chickering and Gamson, 1987,

1991; Husbands and Pearce, 2012; Coe et al, 2014; Greatbatch and Holland, 2016), discussions with samples of teachers including award winners (Skelton, 2004, 2005; Shephard et al, 2010; O'Leary, 2017) or approaches grounded in education theory (Gibbs, 2010; Gunn and Fisk, 2013) allow some tentative conclusions to be drawn. Two of these attempts to define good teaching were developed in relation to teaching in primary and secondary education (Husbands and Pearce, 2012; Coe et al, 2014). It is notable that despite these differences of emphasis, they are nonetheless fairly consistent in the themes that they identify.

The similarities in the conclusions reached are quite striking, if not entirely unexpected. We have grouped the conclusions reached by these studies into five themes. Not all these themes are found in every study, but a majority of these categories are found in all the studies that we listed in the paragraph above. The themes that emerged were discipline mastery, competence in methods of instruction, the use of a range of pedagogies, the quality of interactions between students and teachers, and an understanding of student learning.

The first theme is discipline mastery. It was clearly felt that good teaching requires expertise in the subject(s) being taught, something emphasised in a quite different context by Brookfield (2017). It is interesting to note though that only one study (Coe et al, 2014) lists pedagogical content knowledge as an essential element of discipline mastery. This term, first used by Shulman (1987), refers to the importance not only of subject content but how best to teach it.

All studies identified competence in methods of instruction as an essential element of good teaching. The structuring of sessions, effective use of questioning and assessment for learning, giving of feedback and scaffolding of learning were among the specific techniques listed.

The use of a range of pedagogies was stressed in these studies. These included whole group teaching, active and guided learning, and group learning. The need to create learning environments which were demanding, stimulating and challenging were all identified as being of importance, especially in the communication of high expectations.

The quality of interactions between students and teachers were stressed in many of these studies. This included high levels of student–staff contact, respecting students, recognising their self-worth and identifying their needs, especially in relation to prior learning and taking account of student diversity and a need for equality. The sixth category identified in some of the studies was the importance of an understanding of how students learn, though in some studies this was implicit rather than explicit and only two studies specifically identified the importance of an understanding of learning theory, praxis and practice. Finally, many studies identified the importance of continuing teacher professional development, whether through reflective practice, career-wide learning or SoTL.

In addition to these broad themes, several issues were identified in just one or two studies. These included the importance of stressing to students the importance of their time on task, the need to focus on longer-term learning outcomes and the development of authentic approaches to learning. What was absent from all the studies summarised here was any recognition of the broader scope of teaching in higher education that we will focus on in Chapter 3. Obviously, this is not surprising given that the focus was on good teaching, meaning in this case teaching in the classroom. However, in considering quality in education, the range of other tasks education-focused staff undertake needs to be taken into account. Also, all the studies looked at here pre-date the surge in interest in online, blended, hybrid and hyflex learning stimulated by the Covid-19 pandemic, and the quality of online learning will need to be included in all future discussions.

As part of the personal reflections on their teaching, staff will need to look at what their students would wish to see as part of good teaching. Student feedback comes from student evaluation questionnaires and, in the UK at least, from national surveys of undergraduate students in the final year of their degree programme. However, evidence that systematic biases might exist within this data, especially in relation to the gender or ethnicity of the teachers, challenges its validity. This will be further discussed later in the book. Student-led teaching excellence awards that are organised in many UK universities and the analyses of the reasons that students nominate staff have given us a further valuable source of information about what students perceive as good teaching. (See also our discussion of student-led teaching excellence awards in the next section.) In student feedback, staff often receive praise for personal qualities such as passion, enthusiasm, approachability and organisation.

Teacher excellence

In talking about excellence in teaching, Gunn and Fisk (2013) differentiate between teacher excellence and teaching excellence – the difference being the attributes of excellence exhibited at an individual level as opposed to excellence at the level of a course, programme or institution. While it seems possible to arrive at a consensus on what constitutes good teaching, the idea of what constitutes excellence remains elusive to define. A consensus taxonomy that distinguishes between threshold, quality and teacher excellence has yet to be developed (Gunn and Fisk, 2013). A common thread that often appears in attempts to define teacher excellence is that it involves teachers in going that 'extra mile'. Here we examine critically some of the literature on teacher excellence to summarise what one might expect to see in the teaching by an 'excellent teacher'. The discussion will draw upon a variety of sources, including studies of teaching award programmes, analysis of student-led teaching awards and the higher education literature to try and identify some of those features of excellent teaching.

Student-led teaching awards have grown significantly in number in the last ten years and often involve a number of categories. The commonest are nominations for excellent teaching or pastoral work for students. Student involvement in university teaching excellence awards is also quite common, either as nominators as part of a nominee's application or through having a student as part of the university selection panel. Many student unions carry out analyses of student nominations of staff each year to draw out what students value most from their staff and these are often publicly available. Two of the analyses are examined here, one from Newcastle University (Kara and Barton, 2023) and the other from Edinburgh University Students' Association (2016), together with a report from the Higher Education Academy (Thompson and Zaitseva, 2012). Though separated by an interval of ten years, it is clear that students recognise and seek to reward staff who in their eyes have done something extra. Terms such as dedication, conscientiousness, treating students as individuals, passion, responsiveness and availability occur repeatedly in these reports. This implies that students will readily recognise staff who, in their eyes, have done something extra or additional as part of their teaching (Gunn and Fisk, 2013). More recent work by Lubicz-Nawrocka and Bunting (2019, p 63), exploring student perceptions of teaching, reached broadly similar conclusions in identifying *'concerted visible effort, commitment to engaging students, breaking down student barriers and stability of support'* as being important to students.

What can be learnt about teaching excellence from looking at the criteria employed by internal or national teaching award programmes? The idea of a definition of excellence as going that extra mile often seems explicit in the way the criteria are framed, especially in the case of those awards that involve a competition. Common to many award criteria seems to be a requirement for evidence about personal practice, contributions to the learning of colleagues and active and scholarly reflections. Gunn and Fisk (2013) carried out an analysis of the literature, looking at internal and national award criteria identifying four dimensions of excellence. These were personal practice, assessment, reflective practice and contributions to the profession. The dimension of personal practice includes those qualities valued by students and the practices identified as good teaching in the previous section, along with stimulating critical and scholarly thinking in students. The dimension of assessment includes creative use of feedback and use of a range of assessment methods. Reflective practice includes active engagement with, and acting upon, all sources of feedback from students and from peers. Finally, contributions to the profession include innovation, curriculum development and renewal, contributions from active engagement with professional or disciplinary networks, dissemination of practice through SoTL and leadership of learning and teaching. The implication arising from this classification is that contributions to the profession must always be facing outwards from the institution. This tendency is seen in many national award schemes, and may reflect a tendency to be influenced by criteria for excellence in research.

Going that extra mile is usually implicit in the case of internal processes for personal promotion or advancement. There is an expectation that staff will already be performing at a level above their current grade in order to be considered for promotion to senior lecturer, principal lecturer, assistant or associate professor or a full professor. This applies whether they are an education-focused member of staff or a member of staff where teaching is a part of a mixed portfolio. Usually simply doing a lot of teaching or being a good teacher will not be enough to gain promotion, and we explore this below.

Example 2.1

The UK National Teaching Fellowship Scheme criteria

As an example of award criteria, the UK's National Teaching Fellowship Scheme (Advance HE, 2024) takes a slightly different view. Its three criteria are individual excellence, raising the profile of excellence and developing excellence. To demonstrate individual excellence, nominees are asked to provide evidence of how they enhance and transform student outcomes and/or the higher education teaching profession. Raising the profile of excellence requires applicants to evidence the ways in which they support their colleagues and influence support for student learning and/or the teaching profession, demonstrating impact and engagement going beyond their immediate academic or professional role. Applicants must demonstrate how they develop excellence through their commitment to continuous professional development (CPD) and how this CPD has impacted upon their ongoing practice.

> For each criterion applicants are asked to provide evidence of reach, value and impact. Reach refers to the scale of influence and could be geographic but equally could refer to diverse groups of students or staff. Consequently, value is the benefit felt by students or staff, where those benefits could be locally within a single institution or more widely. Impact is expressed as the difference(s) made to practice, policy and/or student outcomes, and again these could be local but also national or international.
>
> The criteria are scored on a nine-point scale. Each of the three award criteria is given equal weighting in arriving at a final score.

Example 2.1 provides an example of the criteria for a national award scheme, in this case the National Teaching Fellowship Scheme, run by Advance HE for the UK sector. Applicants are asked to provide evidence for each of three criteria. In this example there is a clear sense of the need to go that extra mile to be successful. What sets this scheme apart from many university promotion criteria, for example, is the requirement to demonstrate not just a commitment to professional development but to evidence how that development has influenced ongoing practice.

In summary then, while many might agree that excellence is about that 'extra mile', there is plenty of room for disagreement about what that extra mile involves.

Teaching excellence

As outlined in the section above and in Chapter 1, the drivers for a university to demonstrate excellence in teaching come from several directions. These include the globalisation of higher education and the need to compete for the lucrative international student market. Where students are required to pay a significant part or all of the costs of higher education, then they may also look at the quality of teaching as part of their decision. Finally, for governments the costs of financing higher education are significant and so they will want to ensure value for money.

However, the situation is more complex than that. In the UK it is recognised that teaching quality is only a part of the complex decision regarding choice of university. Other aspects include the availability of a particular course, where to live, the availability of accommodation, perceptions surrounding the quality of student life and finally the perceived prestige of a university, such as its position in world ranking tables or its belonging to a particular prestige group (Blackmore, 2016). Perceived prestige is an important driver, as national governments will often restrict the choices of their students wishing to study abroad by only funding students wishing to study at the more prestigious universities.

The emergence of teaching excellence as a counterbalance to the dominance of research excellence in university rankings is highly problematic. The quotation at the beginning of this chapter makes the critical point that research and teaching are equally important, but it is not saying that they are the same thing. Furthermore, one view of the drive to teaching excellence is that it is a neoliberal strategy for performance management. This risks trivialising teaching by reducing it to an exercise in performativity to achieve high scores in the instruments used to measure teaching excellence, such as student satisfaction. In this view, excellence might be seen as a constantly receding target that can never be attained, rather like the constantly expanding universe. Perhaps a sceptical view of this would have to be that it is a necessary condition of a performativity agenda for teaching – for what use would excellence be if it was attained by all?

Another view of excellence is through the lens of the agenda for parity of esteem in reward and recognition between teaching and research. Reports by Cashmore and Ramsden (2009a, 2009b) highlighted the disparity in reward and promotion for teaching in comparison to research and identified large institutional discrepancies between institutions in the ways in which teaching is considered in reward processes. The view expressed in the reports and by the staff they interviewed was that rewarding and recognising staff was central to obtaining an excellent student experience. In this view, reward and recognition of teaching act to incentivise staff, and the high-quality practice so motivated will result in excellence in their teaching practice. While the equivalence of recognition of teaching and research achievements is a matter of equity and fair practice, a link between reward and recognition of teaching and teaching excellence has been hard to establish. Also, in some institutions, the attempt to ensure rigour in reward mechanisms compared to research can fail to take account of the complexity and diversity of the teaching role in higher education or use measures such as publication of teaching research for which there is little evidence of impact upon teaching practice.

As outlined above and in Chapter 1, ranking tables tend to assume that all universities are similar with similar missions. This is as much of a problem for teaching as it is for research, especially given the diverse nature of the teaching function in universities. Thus, it is misleading to speak of teaching excellence as if it is a universal quality, just as it would be misleading to speak about individual academic staff in such terms. University teaching missions differ considerably as a function of their student recruitment as well as their disciplinary mix. Universities may seek to recruit from their local region with a widening participation agenda. This affects the qualifications expected of students upon entry and may be reflected in lower retention and completion rates. Universities have different disciplinary mixes, with some having a high proportion of disciplines such as medicine, dentistry or law where programmes are overseen by Professional Statutory and Regulatory Bodies (PSRBs). Thus, teaching excellence will mean different things in different institutions, and the aggregation of data that occurs when rankings are compiled masks the granulation of different rankings. It also masks the differences in teaching performance within a university. The Teaching Excellence Framework in England (TEF), introduced to measure teaching quality alongside the longer-established Research Excellence Framework (REF), has attempted to address some of these issues through benchmarking performance indicators; however, attempts to extend this to individual subjects have eluded it.

Teaching excellence is hard to define and some of the mechanisms that seek to establish it risk either trivialising teaching as an exercise or viewing it as equivalent to research, which risks using instruments that are problematic and contested in relation to teaching. A better way forward is one which views education and research as equally important and which uses appropriate forms of evidence of educational achievements that allow judgements to be made with the same rigour as those for research achievements. As with ranking tables more generally, the notion that excellence is a unitary quality is also problematic as university missions and disciplines differ between universities. The diversity of teaching missions in individual universities challenge a universalised idea of teaching excellence and make comparisons of teaching between universities difficult.

Critical issues

Measuring teaching excellence

The contested nature of teaching excellence and the ambiguous nature of the term raise important issues about how one might address questions of its measurement. The use of metrics as outcomes measures might provide one part of the answer but in the light of student perceptions of what constitutes teaching excellence, qualitative process measures might provide more nuanced and relevant information. Using the example of the Teaching Excellence Framework (TEF) in the UK, Gibbs (2016) argues that while some metrics could be used with some confidence, they would alone not be sufficient to make the kinds of decisions the TEF requires. He goes on to argue that process measures, while useful, are not sufficiently developed. Excellence is frequently viewed instrumentally through reward, recognition and advancement, yet at the same time the concept is problematised as being vacuous. It needs to extend beyond the simply performative to embrace a more inclusive approach that extends to including growth and development (Nixon, 2007; Wood and Su, 2017). For Nixon (2007), excellence is not an endpoint but rather a process of continuous growth. The way out of these challenges is explored in more detail in Chapter 4, where a mixed-methods approach supported by a narrative account of teaching achievement is described.

Experts and expertise in teaching

We have seen that teaching excellence, as the term is usually applied, is the result of complex and multiple interactions between the teaching skills of individual staff and the teams and groups they work with. These interactions occur within disciplinary or multidisciplinary teams in the schools or departments of their institutions. Yet amid the drive to number, weigh and measure teaching excellence, the concept remains elusive. At the same time there is an underlying tension in excellence as a concept. This is because of the implication that this drive to excellence is an entity that can be measured and so be present in varying amounts in a university (so many cubits of excellence, one might say), but at the same time it is something that cannot be attained by all and possibly only by a few.

In this narrative only a few teachers in higher education can be considered to be excellent. This idea is encouraged by the plethora of internal and external teaching awards and competitions. At the same time many staff across the whole sector deliver highly effective teaching on a daily basis that leads to high-quality learning and enhanced student outcomes.

One of the consequences of regarding excellence as a goal only attainable by a few is the potential it has to demotivate staff to develop their practice. Reward and recognition and the agenda of parity of esteem have been positioned as one means of motivating staff. In terms of equity between teaching and research, or indeed any other function undertaken by staff, then this is important. However, evidence that equity of reward for staff who teach enhances student outcomes is hard to come by.

Is there another way? Narratives of excellence are also encouraged by the idea that some teachers are naturally gifted and talented, and excellence is the result of innate abilities rather than expertise acquired over time. This kind of view is perhaps more compatible with teacher-centred transmissive conceptions of education rather than an understanding of teaching as a multifaceted professional area of work, whose purpose is supporting students to learn. In a complex learning and working environment like contemporary higher education, it is also hard to believe there is any teacher who cannot continue to develop areas of their practice. Out of these tensions has developed ideas of expertise and expert teachers (King, 2022).

There is a large literature on experts and expertise. Expertness is not simply a state of being but rather a call to action. In other words, it is not something that we naturally have or that we attain and then retain. Rather, the call to action in this case is to constantly seek routes to develop and refine our teaching practice. This involves critically examining evidence about our teaching, experimenting and risk taking in our practice, and engaging and interacting with our students and colleagues. Like excellence, the term 'expert' itself carries a notion of elitism, especially if empirical evidence of what the term means is lacking and instead it is a matter of personal belief and opinion. Experts are simply people who have a high level of knowledge or experience of a topic or field that has been gained over time and which they continue to develop. As Kneebone (2022, p xvi) observes, *'becoming an expert is a path we are all treading and cannot be reduced to the metrics of attainment'*. Becoming an expert teacher involves acquiring knowledge and skills, as well as building experience through reflecting upon the evidence of one's own practice.

The gathering of both quantitative and qualitative evidence, engaging with it and critically reflecting upon it form the subjects of Chapters 4 and 5.

Example 2.2

Case study: Professor Momna Hejmadi

The lack of shared understanding about the nature of teaching achievements is an issue to which we keep returning in this book. This case study demonstrates some of the pedagogical and strategic leadership activities that may feature in an education-focused career in higher education.

Professor Momna Hejmadi was promoted to Professor of Bioscience Education in 2019, was then appointed Associate Dean (Education) and from 2023 has been Associate Pro-Vice Chancellor (Education) at the University of Bath.

Starting as a biomedical scientist in Mumbai, with later international experiences in the US and UK, she has a strong commitment to student-centric approaches to education. As Director of Studies, she led several interdisciplinary, multi-institutional projects which were identified as exemplary in terms of their strong foundations in scholarship, their innovation and practical application, and evidence of impact across the sector. These included the introduction of new programmes and courses, transformative assessment of laboratory practicals using technology, 'blended/flipped' courses, peer assessments, group research projects, use of automated summative assessments for 250+ classes and forging Bath's first highly successful free online course, *Inside Cancer* (2014) and *Understanding and Teaching Evolution* (2018). *Inside Cancer* had over 54k global learners from 149 countries and 36 per cent completion rates in the first three years, demonstrating evidence of a global impact. She has also led departmental strategies to increase recruitment and retention from under-represented as well as international students, which have subsequently been adopted across her faculty.

Momna has influenced policy by serving on many university committees, Council and Senate. As Chair of Bath's 'Resilient Curriculum Project' created in response to the Covid-19 pandemic, she spearheaded the pivot to blended delivery of all institutional taught courses for 2020–21 and, as Associate Dean, led the 'Curriculum Transformation' of all undergraduate and taught postgraduate programmes across five departments. An educational leader within her discipline, she has served on the UK Committee of the Association of National Teaching Fellows and as Editor-in-Chief of *Bioscience Horizons* (Oxford University Press).

She was awarded the prestigious National Teaching Fellowship by Advance HE in recognition of her excellence in teaching and learning. She consistently receives excellent student evaluation scores. She has won three internal awards for teaching, innovation and leadership in education, and consistently receives nominations. She has authored pedagogical publications and delivered keynote seminars nationally and internationally.

Critical issues

Teaching: evidence-based or evidence-informed/evidence-led?

Evidence-based teaching is frequently positioned as a key element in enhancing the quality of teaching in higher education, and evidence from research grounded in theory certainly should be an influence on our teaching practice. Kreber (2013, p 146) suggests a more nuanced approach is necessary, noting that *'a narrow conception of evidence-based practice, however, is founded upon an instrumental rationality that assumes that research evidence once applied to practice will produce predictable results'*.

Certainly, the evidence itself needs to be interrogated to ask questions about the robustness of the evidence, the educational context from which the evidence is drawn, whether the results are relevant to the context or contexts in which they might be used and whether the theoretical framework employed is appropriate. Such an approach might be considered evidence-informed.

Yet to pick up Kreber's argument, the danger is that an evidence-based approach to teaching might be framed as implying that there is a clear and replicable solution for each of our teaching problems, when we know that the success of educational interventions is highly context-specific. Such success depends upon the teacher, the student group, the curriculum and the relationships between them. An over-reliance on evidence-based approaches may further act to stifle our reflections on our own practice. However, as Mann and Walsh (2013) point out, reflective practice can itself be uncritical, lack transparency and not be useable by other practitioners. Thus, it should be data led.

Clearly, a balance needs to be struck between evidence-based and evidence-informed/evidence-led approaches. Perhaps we also need to remember what Brookfield (2017, pp 53–4) tells us, which is that the answer may not always be outside but may lie within ourselves, requiring us *'to research our contexts critically'*.

Critical questions for practice

Teaching 'excellence'

» What would you consider to be excellent teaching in your context?
» Would you be able to distinguish between teaching that was good enough, good or excellent?
» What metrics might you chose to employ to inform a decision about good teaching?
» What qualitative process outcomes would you consider to be appropriate in your context to inform a decision about good teaching?

Summary

- A discourse of 'excellence' in teaching has emerged partly as a counterbalance to similar discourses around research. Concepts of 'excellence' may undermine teaching if not treated critically.

- In a culture of measurement and league tables, there is no straightforward way of measuring teaching quality or defining teaching excellence.

- Analysis of research suggests common themes in what defines 'good teaching'.

- Implicit in definitions of 'excellence' is often the idea of 'going the extra mile', though what this looks like is more contested.

- Expertise, with a focus on constant examination and development of practice, has been proposed as an alternative to excellence.

Useful texts

Gibbs, G (2010) *Dimensions of Quality.* York: Higher Education Academy.

A clear summary overview of key factors in conceptualising and evaluating quality in learning and teaching.

Gunn, V and Fisk, A (2013) *Considering Teaching Excellence in Higher Education: 2007–2013. A Literature Review since the CHERI Report 2007*. Project report. York: Higher Education Academy.

A comprehensive review that critiques both the research and the grey literature on teaching excellence in higher education and problematises concepts of excellence in teaching.

King, H (ed) (2022) *Developing Expertise for Teaching in Higher Education: Practical Ideas for Professional Learning and Development.* Abingdon: Routledge.

A book that arose from a symposium on Expertise in Teaching in Higher Education in 2019. Contributions explore concepts of expertise and what it means to be an expert teacher in higher education from a range of perspectives in thoughtful and provoking ways.

Chapter 3 | Building an education-focused career

Why develop an education-focused career, and what can it look like?

An education-focused career can be extremely rewarding for individuals, as well as beneficial to students, institutions and the sector more widely. However, because the term 'teaching' is widely used to mean any work related to education, there is a common misconception that demonstrating outstanding practice in your own teaching of students is sufficient for promotion and career development. It also implies that this is what an educational career in the higher education sector means. Developing an education career over the long term means going beyond your own teaching practice in some way. In this respect, education careers have similarities with research careers. As well as 'actual' research in the library, archive, field, laboratory or (creative or professional) practice context, academics apply for grants; supervise doctoral students; manage teams; and lead and shape institutional and disciplinary agendas. Similarly, university education is a broad field of work offering opportunities for progression and leadership. The fact that educational career paths tend to be less consistently understood than those relating to research may present challenges when following this career pathway. There are also several common myths about education-focused careers that might discourage some from taking this career path, and these are explored in the 'Critical issues' feature below. Together what this may mean is that you need to think carefully about career as to management and be prepared to advocate more persuasively within your institution the benefits of such a career path (Debowski, 2012; Cleaver et al, 2014; Chalmers, 2021; Smith and Walker, 2021). However, this breadth and flexibility of education-focused careers will be both personally rewarding and bring opportunities of different kinds to those of a research-focused one.

Critical issues

Identifying the myths

One of the challenges in planning a career focused on education is that myths circulate about career possibilities and limitations. It is helpful to identify any common ideas about teaching-focused careers that are current in your context and interrogate them critically, so they are not limiting to individuals or institutions. We share some common ones.

You can't contribute to leadership unless you give up working with students

The number of formal leadership roles in higher education is increasing, and it is true that leadership roles inevitably mean spending some of your time away from direct engagement with students. But there are plenty of leadership roles which enable you to maintain engagement throughout your career, and indeed for many leadership roles continuing contact with students is a vital part of effective leadership. For example, you may retain teaching responsibilities at the level of one or more modules or selected sessions. You may continue to supervise postgraduate students. You may also wish to engage with students in other ways, such as through partnering in research, scholarship and other projects.

Teaching is always a career dead end

Research career pathways are often clearer, research achievements more easily understood and progression can be faster – all of which are important considerations. In a given institution, however, you will find people engaged in educational work at all levels, up to the executive team or equivalent.

Promotion for teaching does not happen, at least not in my university

It is true that some universities are much better than others at promoting on their learning and teaching tracks. This can be due to a misalignment between the promotion criteria and the opportunities available to staff. Learning and teaching criteria may have been devised in a way that mirrors research criteria too strongly. Promotion panels may also interpret educational 'success' in ways that are more suited to research. However, it is also true that academics can be too slow to believe that educational contributions are rewarded (Cashmore and Ramsden, 2009a, 2009b).

Aspects of a teaching career

Career development involves balancing your own strengths, ambitions and areas of interest and expertise with opportunities.

At the outset, building a community around you can be important in several ways:

» learning and contributing to what else is being done in your area of interest;

» finding others to collaborate with;

» understanding which aspects of your own work may be new or distinctive, and therefore of interest to others;

» gaining critical perspectives beyond your own immediate team or institution.

We have broken down the aspects of developing a teaching career into four sections: managing your professional learning and development; individual practice in teaching and/or learning support; leading and co-ordinating practice; and research, enquiry and dissemination of practice.

1. Managing your professional learning and development

University educators often, and increasingly, engage in professional learning and development at the beginning of their careers – for example, by engaging in a Postgraduate Certificate in Academic Practice or equivalent development programme, or gaining recognition through a professional body. While these can form important foundations to professional practice, they are only the first steps for anyone planning to develop their career in this area. Any career presents new challenges and opportunities over time, and new learning is required to fully engage with these. Taking control of your own continuing professional learning and development (CPDL) is also a way of determining, or at least influencing, the nature of opportunities open to you. Without being proactive in terms of career and CPDL planning, you may find your career going in directions you had not intended and opportunities you would have liked to take becoming closed off to you.

Why and how to engage in continuing professional learning and development

It can be easy to think of professional learning and development in terms of specific, organised activities. In fact, it encompasses much more: from informal conversations with colleagues or reading about pedagogy to engaging in educational interest groups within or outside your institution, or within your subject community.

Critical questions for practice

Reflecting on your development

The following reflective questions may help you identify options which are most appropriate for you at a given point in time.

» What are my short-, medium- and long-term career goals and wishes?
» What strengths do I want to build on and develop? Are there gaps in knowledge or skills I want to fill?
» What CPDL do I feel motivated to do? Why?
» What kind(s) of support or resource do I have, such as budget, time flexibility?
» What senior endorsement is helpful or necessary for me to do this?
» Would I prefer my learning in this area to be self-directed or structured?
» Would I benefit from a community of other learners and how will I best find this?
» What problems do I want to solve? What questions do I want to answer?
» How will I benefit from it? Who else will benefit and how – my or others' students, my institutional colleagues, my wider disciplinary colleagues, my institution?

Taking a critical approach to continuing professional learning and development

Much has been written about the centrality of academic disciplines to individual academic identity in higher education (eg Becher and Trowler, 2001). Weller (2019, p 13) notes that:

as disciplinary experts who become teachers, we can be so proficient in using one disciplinary lens that we find it difficult to articulate the intuitive assumptions and decision-making processes that we use when we analyse, select or reject and synthesize complex information about the world around us.

Weller's book advocates developing a critical perspective on learning, teaching and our own development. This can help us avoid becoming trapped in our own unquestioned assumptions. As well as being disciplinary, these may also be grounded in the culture of a particular department or university, a geographical location and context, or an individual's own formative experiences as a learner and teacher.

Brookfield (2017) proposed four 'lenses' through which to reflect on teaching practice. These are students' eyes; colleagues' perceptions; personal experience; and theory. While his original emphasis in offering this model was on using these lenses for professional reflection in a classroom context, this can be a helpful framework in which to consider CPDL more broadly.

Your personal experiences as a learner and teacher – developing an awareness of our own formative experiences and how these have affected our experiences and understanding of learning and teaching – helps us to appreciate our own subjectivity. This in turn can help us to shift our perspective from our own actions as teachers to seeing and responding to the complexity of what is going on for each individual learner as the core problem at the heart of learning and teaching practice (Biggs and Tang, 2022).

The perspectives of students, gathered formally and informally or through our own observations of behaviour and engagement, are thus central to the thinking of anyone who is serious about developing as a teacher in higher education.

The perspective of colleagues, whether gleaned through informal conversations about teaching practice, formal or informal observations, or collaborative working, is another way of getting an alternative view and developing your critical perspective on learning and teaching processes.

Finally, the theory and other pedagogical literature allows you to gain an evidence-informed perspective more rapidly than if you were just relying on your own and colleagues' experiences to develop your understanding.

When engaging in any kind of professional learning and development, you might ask yourself which of these lenses they are enabling you to bring to your practice. Without the challenge of different perspectives, there will be limitations on your professional learning and development. Here are some illustrative examples of professional learning and development. It is not a comprehensive list and other opportunities may very well present themselves depending on your institution and discipline:

» institutional seminars, conferences and discussions on learning and teaching; journal clubs;
» formal development programmes; gaining professional recognition, for example through Advance HE teaching fellowships, the Association for Learning Technology's CMALT Accreditation Framework or the Staff and Educational Development Association's Fellowships Scheme;

- » peer observation schemes and/or mentoring
- » reading pedagogical literature;
- » structured reflection on practice, supported using reflective models; and possibly also going through the process of gaining professional recognition and awards;
- » external assessing or examining or pedagogical consultancy;
- » small research grants, for example Association for Learning Development in Higher Education (ALDinHE); or Staff and Educational Development Association (SEDA).

Many of these opportunities involve networking and meeting people and engaging in professional conversations about learning. As your career develops you may want to network with colleagues outside your institution. External engagement, such as attending and presenting at external learning and teaching conferences, can help you to clarify if what you are doing is particularly original or sector leading, which in turn can boost confidence and internal credibility to influence and lead (see also section 4 below).

2. Individual practice in teaching and/or learning support

Developing your skills, knowledge and expertise as a learning and teaching practitioner is one aspect of career development. This could be as simple as developing more effective ways of teaching in your area(s) of expertise. Indeed, that is the starting point for many. Additionally, it could include: developing expertise in particular aspects of learning and teaching – for example, inclusive assessment; engaging learners from different social and educational backgrounds; decolonisation of the curriculum; or supporting employability. For some, this may be the chief focus of their career. However, career progression normally depends on engagement in one of the two further areas of practice discussed below.

3. Leading and co-ordinating practice

At the smallest scale, this can be module leadership or mentoring new or junior colleagues. More substantial formal leadership roles for academic staff might include Programme Director; Director of Undergraduate or Postgraduate Studies, or Head of Learning and Teaching within a school or faculty; and Head of Department or Subject Area. More senior roles include Head of School or Faculty; and executive roles such as Pro-Vice Chancellor or Executive Dean for Learning and Teaching. There are also roles, such as those of some Associate Deans, with cross-cutting strategic agendas.

Not all leadership depends on formally designated roles in a university hierarchy. You may have a role as a champion of learning and teaching in several ways, for example:

- contributing to, or establishing, professional learning and development activities relating to learning and teaching;
- contributing to, or establishing, mentoring schemes to support learning and teaching careers;
- leading enhancement projects supported by internal or external funding;
- membership of internal groups and committees with a remit to support learning and teaching;
- undertaking, leading or co-ordinating pedagogical research projects;
- developing resources for use in learning and teaching across your institution or for others in your discipline;
- leading on projects that develop your institution's education strategy.

Although there is a hierarchical dimension to these roles, from a career development point of view it is useful to consider the particular skills and knowledge that any given role or opportunity demands, as well as the career possibilities it might open for you. Not all senior roles have line management responsibilities, for example. Some require influencing skills without direct managerial authority. Individuals may be suited to some forms of leadership more than others.

Example 3.1

Case studies: Associate Professors Sue Beckingham and Louise Drumm

These two case studies both feature individuals with expertise in digital and online learning. The first is a subject-based academic with international influence in this area. The second is based in a central learning and teaching department, with a focus on supporting and enhancing academic practice internally, who has also developed a strong profile externally commensurate with her earlier career stage.

This pairing of case studies also highlights the differences in promotion policies and pay structures between institutions. Although both were promoted to Associate Professor, this meant different things in their respective contexts.

For the first, already promoted to Principal Lecturer, it conferred the benefit of increased time for research. For the second, the promotion represented pay progression from the Associate Professor grade.

Case study 1

At the time of Sue Beckingham's promotion from Principal Lecturer to Associate Professor she was nationally, and increasingly internationally, recognised as a leader in the field of the use of social media in learning, teaching and assessment. She was promoted for outstanding contributions to academic leadership and citizenship, and learning and teaching, as well as a significant contribution to research.

As a subject-based academic in computing, Sue had played a significant role within her institution in the leadership of learning, teaching and assessment. Her track record of responsibilities included faculty lead for technology-enhanced learning and degree course leader. She had been the recipient of numerous learning and teaching nominations and awards, internally and externally. She was also a National Teaching Fellow.

She had contributed to several faculty committees related to learning and teaching, as well as several university groups and committees relating to aspects of learning and teaching, including learning analytics and digital learning. Her expertise and influence meant that her role within the institution extended into institution-wide staff development. She established development initiatives, co-wrote social media guidance, facilitated workshops and gave guest lectures across the university.

Her international profile was based on shared practice and innovative approaches in learning, teaching and assessment. This included pioneering and advancing the use of social media and digital technology in learning and teaching. Her research into social media in education is attracting a growing number of citations, and she has led a number of funded projects. Her SlideShare presentations attract a large number of views and downloads.

As well as giving numerous invited keynotes and workshops, Sue contributed to a number of national committees and bodies. Outside these structures, she initiated the Social Media for Learning in HE conference, which has now been successfully established for ten years and is hosted by universities around the UK. In 2014, she co-initiated and, since 2021 has led, LTHE chat – a weekly developmental Twitter (X) conversation bringing together those interested in learning and teaching from across the UK and internationally.

Case study 2

Louise Drumm is an experienced theatre director who came into learning technology after completing a Master's degree in IT software and systems. From there she moved into lectureships in academic development, developing specific expertise in digital and online learning. During this time, she gained a Postgraduate Certificate in Teaching and Learning in Higher Education. In 2018 she completed her PhD in education and technology and moved to a lectureship at a new institution.

By 2019, Louise was an established expert in her field. She rejoined Edinburgh Napier University, where she had worked for several years earlier in her career, in the role of Lecturer in Digital Education. She applied successfully for promotion to Associate Professor in 2021, based on the following achievements.

» In 2020, with the outbreak of the Covid-19 pandemic, she led the Digital Support Partnership to engage staff in using and sharing effective, evidence-informed practice in online learning. To achieve this, she led workshops, a staff network and the creation of podcasts. Measures of student satisfaction and attainment remained constant or improved over this period. The project subsequently won an internal award for its impact.

» Through contributing her expertise to a range of university committees and panels, she has influenced policy and practice across the institution.

» She leads the Academic Practice team, and has been a continuous pedagogical innovator, building internal expertise and capacity through online and face-to-face workshops, teaching and collaborations.

» She also has extensive external engagement, including editorship of a journal; regular invitations as a guest speaker; and national body involvement including chairing conferences and committees. She has been actively publishing and creating and disseminating open resources for a decade.

4. Research, enquiry and dissemination of practice

Dissemination of practice is important for almost anyone developing an education-focused career in higher education. This can take many forms. Healey et al (2020) identify several different genres of writing about learning and teaching, including blogs, opinion pieces and reflective essays. In addition, there are other media and modes of dissemination such as podcasts, digital resources and artefacts, and conference presentations. Disseminating the results of educational enquiry is another form of practice dissemination, and it can lead to networking both within and outside your institution that fosters forms of collaborative enquiry.

If your disciplinary background means that you are not familiar with the methods of educational enquiry, there are issues you are likely to need to consider.

» What can I contribute to educational enquiry? If you have a research background in another discipline, you will have skills, approaches and/or critical frameworks you can bring to an educational research context. Reading educational journals can help you to identify what these might be, and how they can help you to develop your interests. The Society for Research in Higher Education (SRHE) runs workshops on research areas and methods. The SRHE also offers seminars on higher education topics and professional development seminars. There may also be similar opportunities available through your institution or disciplinary or professional body or professional bodies that focus on education such as the British Educational Research Association (BERA). Should you wish to go further, there are a number of programmes of postgraduate study that can help you develop and professionalise your research skills.

» Who can you work with? Undertaking scholarship with others can be an opportunity for educational enquiry that will benefit from the perspectives and knowledge of different researchers working together. For example, if your disciplinary background does not include expertise in educational research methods, then collaborating with a colleague with relevant expertise will be valuable in ensuring methodology that is appropriate and rigorous is employed. An obvious case would be where one researcher has specific skills in qualitative or quantitative research, while another has knowledge of critical or theoretical frameworks or other interpretive approaches. This allows both researchers to learn from each other. A second example would be where you collaborate with colleagues in cognate disciplines, either within your own institution or between institutions, to increase the generalisability of any findings. The term scholarship of teaching and learning – often abbreviated to SoTL – often comes up in discussions of educational enquiry. This term is explored more fully in the 'Critical issues' feature below.

» Where can I start? You could begin with project work within your institution, joining a task and finish group, writing blog posts or attending educational conferences within your institution or nationally, while you build an area of expertise and familiarise yourself with the publication landscape. This could then lead into an enquiry into your own teaching (Wyse et al, 2018), collaborations with colleagues or work with colleagues in other institutions.

Critical issues

What is scholarship of teaching and learning (SoTL) and is it a helpful term?

The term scholarship of teaching and learning – often abbreviated to SoTL – is frequently used in the context of educational enquiry. However, its definition is contested, and some feel it is unhelpful. As Smith and Walker (2021, p 2) highlight, *'the evaluation of scholarship activity does not yet have established sector norms'*. Broadly speaking, SoTL is understood as enquiry into learning and teaching practice, with the aim of enhancing practice for the enquirer and more widely.

As Fanghanel et al (2016) point out, defining SoTL is fraught with the same ambiguity and confusion as defining higher education teaching itself. Even the term 'scholarship' on its own is problematic: it is often used to mean scholarly activity that does not fit the category of original research. This is unhelpful to individuals, whose job interviewers may not understand the term and may not realise that their work involves research. It also means that, even where it forms part of the criteria for promotion, there may be widely varying conceptualisations of its meaning across everyone involved – promotion applicants, panel members, academic leaders and line managers, and human resources colleagues. In addition, the inconsistencies may make moving to roles in other institutions problematic (Smith and Walker, 2021). In the UK, the Research Excellence Framework (REF), a national research evaluation exercise which allocates research ratings and funding to universities, does not fully recognise pedagogical research (Cotton et al, 2018). This lack of clarity around the scope of SoTL and its status raises further questions over its recognition: should enquiry into the practice of an individual be put on a par with 'research'? If not, where does 'SoTL' end and 'research' begin?

These questions aside, writing and publishing on learning and teaching has particular characteristics. Notably, it tends to range over wider areas than disciplinary research (eg Cotton et al, 2018). Secondly, aside from the generic learning and teaching journals, there are also journals for specific academic disciplines.

Some practice-based journals have consciously supportive editorial processes, which can be especially helpful to those stepping outside their usual research paradigm to write about their educational practice.

» The journal *Teaching in Higher Education* has a supportive process, ensuring the development of promising submissions needing further work and supporting access to research journals for scholars from the global south.

» The *Journal of Multidisciplinary Graduate Research* is designed to support Master's and doctoral students beginning to publish peer-reviewed work.

» *Practice and Evidence of the Scholarship of Teaching and Learning in Higher Education* (PESTLHE) aims to publish small-scale practitioner research and case studies of practice, focused on student learning and informed by relevant literature. It is open to contributions that involve reflection, critique and implications for future practice.

» Other journals, such as *Practice: Contemporary Issues in Professional Learning*, consider forms of contribution in the field of higher education beyond empirically researched articles, such as reflective accounts of practice.

There are also channels of pedagogical dissemination outside the parameters of traditional peer-reviewed journals (see Healey et al, 2020). While these may not always have the prestige of journal publications, they may be more widely read and support your career development in other ways. Such publications, including guest posts on high-profile blogs, or pedagogical reports or resources available online via the websites of educational institutions or national bodies, are often more easily accessed and shared. They may consequently have greater impact on others' practice than a peer-reviewed article.

Issues and considerations in developing your teaching career

Because of the context we have already described, there are particular issues to consider.

- » Career structures and pathways. Increasingly, there are academic career tracks in universities which recognise educational contributions. These can be variable in their effectiveness. The expectations of these career tracks can also vary widely between institutions due to the lack of a consistently understood career framework, as we have discussed in Chapter 1. Activities that might open up opportunities and promotion in some institutions and areas of work might not in others. To manage your career well, you need to understand the internal and external landscapes: internal and external mentors can be useful here: for example, a senior colleague who can give you insight into your own institutional context; and people who can help you situate your career in a wider sector context.

- » The need for specialised mentoring and networks. For many, colleagues in their own institution form the basis or starting point for their own learning and teaching community. However, this is not always the case. Some institutions and departments are small, and higher education is by its nature specialised. You may belong to a disciplinary specialism that is unique in your institution, or have interests or expertise in highly specialised aspects of higher education. In these situations, it is possible to be surrounded by supportive colleagues but be professionally and intellectually quite isolated. This can in turn restrict your development and your awareness of the opportunities available to you. Consequently, building links with colleagues outside your institution, while usually helpful, can be vital in these situations.

- » Engaging internally or externally is likely to mean being proactive and identifying your own development needs. It may be that there isn't anyone within your institution who can tell you where to look to find the right mentors and role models and understand the opportunities available to you. You may need to first identify opportunities for external engagement, such as identifying relevant conferences and networks to attend, and build some connections. Clinical and other vocational disciplines tend to be well served by professional bodies with involvement in learning and teaching agendas. In other disciplines, what organisations there are and how active they are can vary widely.

» The evolving higher education landscape and opportunities. Higher education is changing and expanding all the time. This can create uncertainty and instability, for example due to changes and reductions in levels of government funding. It also creates more, or different kinds of, opportunities – such as those relating to international partnerships and emerging private providers. Your career planning may need to be flexible to account for unknown future changes.

» What are the accepted truths around teaching careers and progression in your institution?

» Where might you find the information you need to test how truthful they really are in your own institution and/or disciplinary context?

Summary

- Higher education learning and teaching careers encompass a range of contributions, including scholarship, leadership and external engagement.
- Being proactive about professional learning and development and external engagement is likely to be an important aspect of your career development.
- Understanding the landscape and keeping up to date with changes and developments in your institutional and wider disciplinary/professional contexts can be important in managing a learning and teaching career.

Useful texts

Brookfield, S D (2017) *Becoming a Critically Reflective Teacher*. 2nd ed. San Francisco, CA: Jossey-Bass.
This book remains an invaluable source for starting to think critically about teaching.

Smart, F and Popovic, C (2021) *Educational Developers Thinking Allowed*. [online] Available at: https://edta.info.yorku.ca (accessed 11 March 2024).
This virtual book is a useful orientation for those establishing themselves in the field of educational development.

Weller, S (2019) *Academic Practice: Developing as a Professional in Higher Education.* London: SAGE Publications.

In this book, Weller sets out to support academic professional learning and development in learning and teaching in higher education, particularly through a critical stance on learning and teaching. It is recommended for anyone beginning to develop their expertise in learning and teaching. It also contains a very useful short introduction to enquiry-based approaches to learning and teaching.

Chapter 4 | Evidencing the effectiveness of teaching

In this chapter, we critically examine the practicalities of evidencing teaching and some of the theoretical issues that arise when using particular forms of teaching evidence. There are several reasons why you as an individual might want to evidence the effectiveness of your teaching – for example, to support an application for a teaching award, promotion or for recognition through the Advance HE Professional Standards Framework (PSF) (Advance HE UK, 2023a), a widely recognised framework for benchmarking success within higher education teaching and learning support. Evidence might be needed to support a case for curriculum enhancement, the monitoring of teaching quality or for programme review or external accreditation. Finally, you might simply want to gather evidence about your teaching for purposes of personal development. Whatever the reason, the evidence to be gathered is likely to involve a mixed-methods approach, blending quantitative and qualitative data. This is because teaching is heavily dependent on contextual factors: the students; the individual teacher; and factors affecting the learning environment including class sizes, access to learning resources and the nature of the programme and institution. These numerous variables, which are themselves constantly shifting, mean that no single piece of evidence alone can be meaningful. Instead, evidence being used for any given purpose needs to come from several sources. The precise kinds of evidence you need are also highly contextual. They could be categorised into those which are gathered personally, evidence from sources within the institution and external sources. To make an effective case, you will need to critically evaluate the evidence available to select what is most valuable and appropriate and to ensure it is sufficiently triangulated – that is, that you are not over-reliant on a single, limited piece of evidence to support a particular claim. Ideally, to be effective as a developmental tool, evidencing teaching should become an active and ongoing part of your everyday practice and professional reflection.

In this chapter, rather than being prescriptive about what evidence to use, we will explore these contested issues critically. The aim is to support you to identify and reflect on the complexities of evidencing teaching, enabling you to arrive at conclusions for action that are appropriate and effective for your context.

Why might we need to evidence teaching effectiveness or teaching quality?

Being able to evidence teaching achievement is important for several purposes. Effective evidencing of teaching will be needed when making a case for reward or recognition of your contributions to teaching, whether through promotion or for internal or external teaching award applications such as the National Teaching Fellowship Scheme (NTFS) run in the UK (Advance HE, 2023b) or other similar schemes run in other parts of the world (eg the Australian Awards for University Teaching, 2021 and Society for Teaching and Learning in Higher Education Awards, 2021). Reviewing evidence about teaching effectiveness is also an important precursor of any review of curriculum, as well as providing ongoing evidence of the impact upon student outcomes of changes to teaching programmes. Teaching evidence will need to be assembled as part of any quality assurance process, whether as part of regular internal monitoring, periodic programme validation or as part of an external review such as those carried out by professional, statutory or regulatory bodies. An important part of evidencing teaching is the process of self-reflection on your own teaching. This is needed for ongoing professional learning (CPDL) and can also be used in an application for recognition through schemes such as the Professional Standards Framework (PSF) run by Advance HE (Advance HE, 2023a) or as part of an external appraisal or validation process to continue to practise as an educator. In these latter two contexts there can be particular value in viewing evidence collection as not just a performative task to fulfil the requirements but as a means to develop your own teaching, the educational practices of your institution or to contribute to wider conversations about teaching in higher education. Cashmore and her colleagues, in a series of reports for the Higher Education Academy, identified the importance of rewarding and recognising teaching as a means of enhancing teaching within an institution (Cashmore and Ramsden, 2009a, 2009b; Cashmore et al, 2013). We explore the importance of evidence in this context in Chapter 7.

The ability to evidence the effectiveness of teaching is thus an important aspect of teaching practice that it is easy to overlook or put to one side. This is partly because gathering evidence about your teaching takes time and in a busy teaching schedule this is not always easy to find. It is also because evidencing teaching is often viewed as 'difficult' or sometimes even impossible to achieve. It is true that it is not without challenges. These arise from several sources. We are operating in a metrics-driven context where the apparent certainty of quantitative data tends to be privileged over the richness and complexity of the qualitative. Yet quantitative data alone is ill-suited to addressing the diverse, changing and social nature of teaching in higher education, as well as its context dependency. Consequently, there is a need for mixed methods approaches to address both the 'what' and the 'why' of your evidence, along with a requirement to deploy evidence for purposes which may be either criterion- or norm-based. Constructing an effective case thus depends on a narrative approach to presenting these multiple sources of evidence. While you may be comfortable writing about yourself in this way, it is not something that sits comfortably with everyone's values and identities. These issues of narrative and its challenges are more fully explored in Chapter 5. There are also other challenges.

Firstly, the nature of teaching in higher education is far more diverse than is sometimes portrayed. As we described in Chapter 2, teaching in higher education is about much more than classroom or online teaching practice (Academy of Medical Sciences, 2014) but includes teaching leadership – formal and informal – as well as strategic leadership within and beyond the institution. Each of these modes or genres of practice presents challenges when it comes to evidencing achievement, especially in the case of teaching leadership (Fung and Gordon, 2016).

Secondly, unlike research, evidence of an individual's teaching achievements will not usually be in the public domain. Publications in academic journals or monographs in the grey literature, perhaps as reports, working papers or evaluations, will be accessible. Also accessible will be information about externally or internally funded teaching grants and awards. Internally there is likely to be some information from student evaluations, as well as that which you actively gather yourself.

Thirdly, adapting evidence to specific purposes is an art in itself. In many situations – such as submitting a claim for PSF recognition or (usually) for promotion – applications are criterion referenced. However, in applications for teaching awards that are to be judged competitively, for example, there will be an element of norm referencing. External fellowships, where only a limited number of awards may be given in any one round, are a good example of this. It is usually accepted that other applicants close to the boundary might also have been worthy winners.

Finally, where you are working in a team, you will need to judge and discuss your contribution and those of other team members. These challenges influence the way in which you will choose to present your evidence (see Chapter 5) and may also influence how you choose to gather it and how it is ultimately viewed by readers.

What is the nature of teaching evidence?

As we have explored above, quantitative data in the form of numerical evaluation scores, for example, is often more effective as evidence when supported by qualitative free text comments from students, peers and internal or external assessors. The quantitative data will tell you the 'what' about your teaching and the qualitative evidence will tell you the 'why' (Baumfield et al, 2012). Effective evidencing of teaching thus involves a skilful blending of quantitative and qualitative data to produce an evidence-supported narrative of your teaching achievements.

There has been, and in many places continues to be, a bias towards the gathering of quantitative data such as the results of student surveys, student outcomes or student destination data, including student incomes at defined times after graduation. This kind of quantitative data has a seductively transparent quality. Numbers can be compared; league tables can be drawn up or defined thresholds of quantitative achievement set. We know of departments compiling league tables of staff based on student evaluations and posting these publicly. Student evaluation scores for staff are sometimes used, in the US for example, when making decisions about staff reward or advancement (see also Chapter 2).

The difficulty with an over-reliance on quantitative data is that there is always a need for context when reaching a decision about the reliability of that data. For example, student evaluation data has been criticised on the grounds that race and gender of academic staff can affect student assessments of teaching (Hoorens et al, 2021; Daskalopoulou, 2024). Though a recent paper has challenged this view (O'Donovan, 2024), it is generally accepted that there is a strong possibility of bias affecting student evaluations of teaching, which has led a number of universities in the UK to review whether these evaluations should be collected, and if so how they are used. It is also sometimes said that it is easier to gain higher scores for a final-year optional module, for example, than a first-year compulsory one (Brennan and Williams, 2004). Student assessment outcomes, often proposed as another quantitative measure of teaching effectiveness, have been criticised on the basis that they fail to take account of prior achievement by students in a cohort – a strong predictor of student success (Gibbs, 2010, 2012). Measurement of learning gain has been suggested as a way of accounting for these differences in student achievement but reliably quantifying this is fraught with difficulties (Kandiko Howson and Buckley, 2020). Likewise, graduate earnings are not a simple quantitative measure, as they depend upon factors including the subject mix in a university and issues of prestige and cultural capital accruing to particular institutions (Brink, 2018). These last three issues and their possible impact upon reward and recognition of teaching within institutions are also discussed in Chapter 7.

This is not to say that quantitative data is without value. Properly contextualised, student evaluation scores and student assessment outcomes provide valuable feedback to staff on how their teaching is being received, and how it might be developed – particularly in relation to topics that students find difficult. Metrics about pedagogical research funding or publication may also be relevant. A member of staff might be the recipient of student, institutional or external teaching awards.

However, this data needs to be triangulated (eg Bamber, 2013). This simply means combining it with data from other sources, or using complementary methods, to reduce bias and ensure any conclusions drawn are based on more robust evidence (Noble and Heale, 2019). Two examples of potential qualitative data are the free text comments or reviews from students gathered as part of surveys; and student focus groups, which can provide richer data. Both sources need to be managed carefully to ensure fair representation of the views shared. Focus groups are also time-consuming to set up and analyse and are often reserved for situations such as preparing for a major curriculum review, where the time involved can be justified in terms of the longer-term goals. Quick and simple forms of qualitative feedback gathered while a course is in progress may in many contexts be more valuable and practical than both of these (see 'The sources of evidence' later in this chapter). Such feedback can counter the 'post-mortem' nature of data gathered in student evaluation questionnaires after a course has been completed, which only benefits succeeding cohorts. There is a particular value to methods of gathering feedback which are more collaborative. For example, you could ask students one or two key questions – *'What did you value about this course?' 'What would you like to change?'* – and leave the room while they discuss them. They can then present their collective responses to you when you return, so that they are not directly attributable to anyone, and you can have a richer discussion (Brookfield, 2017).

Students are not the only source of qualitative feedback. Peers can provide valuable insights to colleagues through peer observation of teaching practice or materials, especially if they are asked to focus on aspects of practice a member of staff has themselves identified as problematic or otherwise important to explore (Jarvis and Clark, 2020). Senior colleagues, and external examiners and assessors, can be valuable sources of evidence about teaching in the form of comments in internal or external reviews of programmes or in external examiners' reports. Peer review (as opposed to peer or developmental observation of teaching) has been proposed as another source of evidence of teaching achievement. We examine this critically in Chapter 7 in our discussion of institutional processes. Some teaching award schemes, most frequently student-led awards, provide staff with qualitative feedback alongside the award itself.

The issue with all such forms of qualitative feedback is that all too often its value is contested because it is viewed as subjective in comparison to quantitative teaching metrics or those used to assess research performance. However, even in research it is being seen that there is a need to look beyond the metrics, with an increasing emphasis being placed on the impact on the field or stakeholders (eg Bornmann, 2017; Index of revisions to the 'Guidance on submissions' 2019/01 REF 2021, 2020).

Where does the evidence come from?

As the role of educators in higher education continues to broaden beyond simply teaching online or face to face, evidence of teaching achievement also needs to broaden to gather sources of evidence of achievement within those wider education functions. One lens through which to view and consider where sources of evidence might be sought is from the Advance HE Promoting Teaching project document *Making Evidence Count*, in which one of this book's authors – Steve – was involved as a co-author. This was a guide to evidencing teaching achievement (Advance HE, 2013c). Though it was developed to support evidencing teaching achievements in relation to promotion, the framework for evidence which it sets out has proved valuable in other contexts. The framework classifies teaching activities according to three perspectives: the scope of activity (what teachers do); sphere of influence (the impacts that teachers have within and beyond their institutions); and sources of evidence, including how these change across the course of a career. You may find these a useful way to understand and map out what evidence you need for a given purpose. Because of this, we use the framework to structure our discussion of evidencing below.

Scope of activity

Under scope of activity, the framework lists five areas of activity: professional learning, student engagement, curriculum development, research and scholarship, and leadership and collaboration. As the last chapter explored, staff who teach in universities need to undertake professional development as part of developing their careers. Staff will be engaging with students directly through face-to-face and online learning and teaching activities, assessment and feedback, academic and pastoral support, and undergraduate and postgraduate supervision (Light et al, 2009). Teachers will be expected to be involved in curriculum development at module and programme level to support curriculum coherence and adherence to internal and external quality frameworks and the requirements of professional bodies. Curriculum development will also include identification or development of learning and teaching resources.

In an educational context, research and scholarship includes knowledge of both generic and subject-specific pedagogy (Shulman, 1987). It might also include dissemination to groups within your discipline internally at school or faculty level, at institutional learning and teaching conferences, and external presentations to other institutions, education conferences or professional societies. Some staff may engage in research, possibly supported by internal or external grants. This will often be in the form of close-to-practice research (Wyse et al, 2018) but may involve internal or external collaborations. Finally, teaching staff will engage in leadership at a variety of levels. At the start of a career this could simply mean leadership of their students or peer-to-peer support and mentoring. In the later stages of a career this could extend to mentoring of staff, course governance up to programme level or involvement in quality assurance and programme accreditation.

Pedagogical scholarship is sometimes referred to as 'scholarship of teaching and learning' (SoTL). As we discussed in Chapter 2 and as Gunn and Fisk (2013) observe, there is a degree of complexity as to what the term SoTL means. This means it is not always a helpful term when developing a shared understanding of pedagogical scholarship within institutions, though the international SoTL movement (ISoTL) has made the concept more understandable to the wider community. For a further discussion of this issue see the 'Critical issues' feature in Chapter 3.

You may have achievements which draw on evidence from all five of these areas of activity. For example, professional development may have an impact on teaching practice and curriculum development. This may then lead to research and leadership which has a different kind of impact. This and other issues around presenting your evidence are fully explored in Chapter 4.

Sphere of influence

Sphere of influence defines the levels of involvement staff have more broadly within and outside their institution. Scope of activity refers principally to activities within a course, module or programme. Sphere of influence refers to staff involvement across programmes within their institution beyond teaching but through contributions to the wider learning and teaching agenda. The framework in *Making Evidence Count* breaks this down by defining three levels of influence that teaching staff might have beyond the direct impacts on the students they teach. The first level is within a school or faculty but beyond the programmes on which they teach. The second level of influence is within the university, across schools and faculties, in interdisciplinary or more strategic activities. The third level of influence a teacher might have is that which extends beyond their institution. At the early career level this might be simply as a team member but later could include leadership of committees or groups. Sphere of activity could then extend to roles such as an external examiner or external advisor working as a member of external groups such as external accreditation bodies, professional societies, or industry or government bodies nationally or internationally. Taken together, these spheres of influence represent a very wide range of possibilities.

As with scope of activity, you may find that mapping out your achievements in relation to their sphere of influence is a useful starting point. This is explored further in Chapter 5.

Example 4.1

Case study: Professor David Rose

David Rose is an academic in the field of philosophy. Prior to his professorial promotion, he had demonstrated significant internal impact plus a substantial track record of pedagogical scholarship with a strong citation record.

David has promoted a values-led approach to learning within his discipline, in which learning is determined by students' interests and understood as reciprocal. For example, students on his programme engage in research and publication. This approach also emphasises the importance of links to contemporary issues: students report that they graduate understanding their education as relevant to the wider world and their employment context. His courses are noted for high student engagement; excellent NSS scores; and students outperforming those on comparable programmes elsewhere. He has received repeated commendations from external examiners and internal review panels. More formal recognition of teaching excellence and innovation, over two decades, has included numerous internal student-led and other award nominations; receipt of two university prizes; and a National Teaching Fellowship.

In addition to his scholarship, David has promoted his pedagogical approaches through leadership within his university. As Head of Department, he has built up his subject area and programmes, including recruitment, mentoring and development of a new team. They in turn have been shortlisted for, and won, multiple awards, both collectively and individually. His contribution to faculty leadership supported development of thinking around learning and teaching beyond his subject area. This has resulted in direct and indirect impact on practice elsewhere in his institution. This impact is replicated more widely at other institutions nationally, and he is engaged in international project leadership in partnership across several countries.

Sources of evidence

If the range of activities outlined above are all examples of possible activities that teaching staff can be involved in, and this list is not exhaustive, then where should staff be looking in terms of evidence? The framework considers three main sources of evidence that can contribute to a narrative about teaching achievement: personal reflection, students and peers. The weight given to these sources of evidence is likely to change as a teaching career develops. Early in a career, evidence may be drawn largely from personal reflection and from students, but at later stages of a career, if the sphere of influence widens, that evidence would come increasingly from peers.

Evidence from students

We have already mentioned some of the kinds of evidence relating to students, including quantitative and qualitative student feedback, assessment results and destination data, but there are others. Surveys looking at how students engage in their learning have tended to be confined to an institutional level but there is no reason why smaller-scale surveys cannot be conducted at the level of a programme or year of study. Student engagement data can also be gathered from virtual learning environments. Assessment results give quantitative information on student outcomes with the caveat noted above. Examination of written work by external examiners or through peer review can be a valuable source of qualitative information on the depth and quality of student learning. Student prizes or success in national competitions or contributions to national student research conferences might also be relevant for certain programmes. Student-led teaching awards, which have become widespread in the UK, constitute a further evidence source.

Despite its perceived shortcomings, quantitative student evaluation data is widely used in evidencing teaching achievements. There is a significant literature on this topic, which we draw upon throughout this book. *Collecting and Using Student Feedback* (Brennan and Williams, 2004) remains a valuable source of guidance on the crucial issues of design and use of questionnaires, even though the technology around collecting the data has moved on significantly since that study was published. The debates around how to collect and use the data are many and varied. Issues include how to frame the questions; how many numbers (even or odd) form the Likert scale; how to express the results from a scale that is not linear; and what level of participation is needed for reliability. There are no right or wrong answers here and views differ among researchers. Two further issues have come to the fore in recent years. The first is the fall in participation rates by students reported by many institutions, especially when data is collected in online surveys. The second is evidence of discrimination in surveys as pointed out above, resulting in lower scores being obtained by younger staff, female staff or Black, Asian and Minority Ethnic (BAME) staff, which has led some institutions to abandon this form of gathering student opinion (eg Fan et al, 2019). The dangers of relying on quantitative data alone are obvious. The importance of triangulation of this source of data with data from other sources has been outlined above. We revisit these issues in Chapter 5, along with the importance of providing a context for critical interpretation of the data when developing a narrative about teaching achievement.

As mentioned above, another key issue is when to administer questionnaires. Frequently, this is done at or near the end of a course. Others have proposed a more developmental and light-touch approach. One favoured approach is a mid-term evaluation. An example of this would be a 'traffic light' approach, asking questions about teaching with the option of green, amber or red as a response. Green would mean do not change this aspect of the course, red would mean stop doing something and amber would mean change something that you are doing (Race, 2001; Exley and Dennick, 2009). There are several other approaches to gathering student opinion which have been found to be quick and successful. These include 'ticket out of class', where students are invited to complete a quick quiz or answer one question, such as: What is the key idea you are taking away with you from this session? or Which concept would you like to know more about before leaving the class? The results are then used by the teacher to frame a discussion at the start of the next session. Group discussion methods such as World Café can be used to gather student opinion, including at the start of a course as part of induction and to gain valuable perceptions of their expectations (Wakeling et al, 2016; The World Café, 2022).

Qualitative feedback from students can be used alone or to supplement quantitative data. Here, online surveys are helpful as – despite lower participation rates – the experience of many has been that online questionnaires can be sources of richer free text comments from students than surveys that are paper based. A more intensive way to gather this kind of data would be the use of focus groups. This could require the use of trained facilitators and the data is more time-consuming to analyse. For this reason, as pointed out above, such an approach is more suited to higher-stakes situations such as prior to a major restructuring of a programme.

Evidence from peers

The second source of evidence is peers, possibly in the form of peer observation of teaching. A difficulty here can arise because of the multiple potential uses of peer observation data. Observation of teaching can be used as a means of quality assurance – that is, to check the teacher is doing a 'good-enough' job – but the value of such approaches has been critiqued by many as being driven by a performative rather than developmental agenda (O'Leary, 2017; Jarvis and Clark, 2020). Peer observation can also be used purely developmentally. The evidence is that this works best in low-stakes peer-based approaches as they lead to more dialogic and developmental discussions (O'Leary, 2017; Jarvis and Clark, 2020). There are also more formal processes of peer review of teaching in which a member of staff, usually senior, comes into a classroom to view a teaching episode which can then be used as evidence in a promotion application. In the latter case, the question arises as to who owns the data. An approach used by the University of Wollongong involved establishing a panel of reviewers, one of whom could be invited to review a teaching episode and then provide evidence to the teacher. The resulting evidence remained the property of the teacher, who could choose whether or not to use it in an application for advancement (Sandra Wills, personal communication). Clearly, the uses of evidence from peer review of teaching vary according to how it was gathered and the teacher's and reviewer's perspectives on what constitutes good teaching (Jarvis and Clark, 2020).

Effective mentoring of colleagues can be evidenced by comments from mentees though consent to share, and other issues of confidentiality and probity will need to be respected, including how power relationships might make more junior staff feel obliged to comment positively. What other forms of evidence might be available will depend on the nature of the contribution(s) that an individual is making to the learning and teaching agenda of their institution. Recognition of teaching achievement in relation to teaching within a programme might come from a head of school or department or a programme leader. Evidence supporting effective contributions to the work of committees or projects might come from the chair of that committee or task and finish group. Evidence of the effectiveness of work undertaken to lead such a group – for example, chairing a board of studies or leading a university review of assessment – might need to come from a senior manager in the university. As with evidence from students, evidence from peers might also come in the form of an award from an institutional awards scheme.

Evidence from external recognition

A third source of evidence is external recognition from peers. Esteem indicators such as invitations to deliver workshops, speak at learning and teaching conferences, join or chair national groups, act as an editor or associate editor of learning and teaching journals, or to be an honorary officer of a professional body or society would all indicate peer recognition beyond the institution. External teaching grant funding and pedagogical publication are further important esteem indicators. Finally, success in a national teaching award scheme would be another form of external peer recognition, as would achievement of the higher categories of the PSF 2023, especially Principal Fellowship of the Higher Education Academy (PFHEA) for which evidence of effective strategic leadership is required. We explore how institutions recognise the value of these in Chapter 6.

A particular issue with evidence from peers, whether those contributions are internal or external to the institution, relates to working in teams. So much educational activity involves work in teams of varying sizes, and in these cases there is always a need for you to be clear what your particular contribution has been.

Another model to use when considering evidence of teaching achievement has been developed for the Royal Academy of Engineering by Ruth Graham (2015, 2018), as a means to promote greater recognition of teaching and its reward through promotion for academic engineers. The project has now acquired an international dimension, the Advancing Teaching project. The Royal Academy of Engineering in the UK has been a major project sponsor, along with other sponsors including the 4TU Centre for Engineering Education and the Dutch Ministry for Education, Culture and Science University Teaching. In this context, the resulting Career Framework for University Teaching offers *'both a structured pathway for academic career progression and an evidence base on which to demonstrate and evaluate teaching achievement'* (Advancing Teaching, 2024). It built on existing understanding and knowledge, including Advance HE's *Making Evidence Count*, to create *'a resource that universities can adapt to their academic career structures and progression points'* (Advancing Teaching, 2024). The framework and its associated resources, are an example of career development support within a particular discipline – in this case, engineering. Large parts of it are nonetheless more broadly applicable, as evidenced by it forming the foundation of the multidisciplinary, international Advancing Teaching project (Advancing Teaching, 2024).

Example 4.2

How is teaching evidence gathered?

One of the consequences of teaching roles in higher education being so diverse is that evidence of teaching achievements will come from multiple sources and be gathered in different ways. These have been explored above and are listed in Table 4.1.

Table 4.1 Possible sources of evidence for teaching achievements

Evidence often held by universities	Evidence held externally	Evidence you need to gather yourself
Internal teaching grants	External teaching grants	Targeted evidence from students relating to specific aspects of learning and teaching
Postgraduate taught and doctoral supervision numbers and completions	External roles, eg external examining, roles with professional bodies, external reviewing, work on external groups and committees	Mid-course or informal student evaluation
Undergraduate project supervisions		Peer observation
Records of peer-reviewed publications, books, book chapters and other forms of publication		Other external activities, eg presentations, workshops
Student evaluations of modules and programmes		Collaborative teaching projects and contributions to university groups and committees
Student assessment outcomes		
Student destination data		

Critical issues

Individual contributions in teams

Gathering evidence about teaching effectiveness when working in a team as a member or as its leader

Often much of the work that we do as teachers involves working in teams. Teams can be very small. An obvious example is team teaching in pairs. As Brookfield (2017, p 66) observes, *'to have a colleague who helps you debrief the class you have just taught and who alerts you to things (positive and negative) you've missed is extremely helpful for your own efforts to check your assumptions about what's happening'*. Evidence from our peers is one of Brookfield's four lenses of critical reflection (Brookfield, 2017).

Often though we will be working in larger teams, either as a member with a defined role or acting as leader of the whole team or leading part of its work. For example, a major review of a degree programme or a curriculum may require a large team. This could involve several stages: initial consultations with staff and students; possibly some co-creation with students, depending on the programme consultation with the relevant Professional Statutory and Regulatory Body (PSRB); curriculum design; design of assessment structures; managing the course approval processes; and then an implementation phase, perhaps with further staff consultation.

There are awards which recognise teams for their achievements. In such cases, the application will be free to explore the impact of these achievements without attributing them to an individual – though there may be a requirement to explore how the team has worked together. As higher education staff though, if we are to claim individual credit for our teaching effectiveness when working with a team, perhaps as part of a case for advancement through promotion, then we need to be clear what our distinctive contribution to the work of that team has been. This is especially important if other team members might also be seeking promotion or advancement and using their work within the same team as part of a promotion case within the same round. It is best if this is agreed at the outset and kept under review. This should include an open discussion, which ensures all project members – irrespective of their level of seniority – are fully valuing their contribution, aware of its potential career benefits and supported to self-advocate. There may also be a strategy for undertaking research as part of a project with the intention of disseminating the results internally or externally. Again, the importance of deciding the attribution of credit and doing so in advance is extremely important (Brand et al, 2015; Allen et al, 2019).

The challenges to doing this are not dissimilar to the challenges faced in attributing credit to colleagues engaged in large research projects. Many universities now have attribution of good research practice and authorship policies which, while obviously written more with disciplinary research in mind, could provide a template for education projects. The key principle is to agree the attribution of credit at the outset.

Gathering good quality evidence

For many teaching activities, evidence needs to be collected at the time. Consequently, it is necessary to build evidence gathering into an activity such as a workshop or seminar. This might include not just asking participants for feedback immediately after the event but also going back to them after a suitable interval to ask whether they have incorporated any ideas from your event into their own practice. It is no good delivering, for example, a series of workshops on an educational innovation to a series of national audiences and then seeking to gather evidence of their influence on practice five years later. It needs to be done at the time and then – depending on the kind of impact for which evidence is being sought – followed up at suitable intervals to assess longer-term impact. What we are arguing here is that evidence gathering must be an active process, and as such it is something that does not necessarily sit comfortably with education-focused staff.

Gathering evidence from peers about teaching achievement can feel particularly uncomfortable. You could be lucky in having an external examiner or reviewer comment specifically about an aspect of your teaching, but more often such comments will have to be purposively sought. You might, for example, approach the chair of a committee of which you are a member, or a senior manager who knows your work, to ask them to provide a quote or statement which summarises your contribution to an activity within or outside your institution. In practice, most colleagues will be only too happy to provide a comment or judgement about an aspect or aspects of your work – and may put more effort into it than you anticipated. Such comments are especially valuable for staff in leadership roles where it is also possible to undertake limited forms of 360-degree feedback. These comments can offer opportunities for learning as sometimes our knowledge of the impact of our work can be tacit rather than explicit (Atkinson and Claxton, 2000).

As well as gathering the evidence, you will need to retain it in a useful form. This involves compiling some kind of personal teaching portfolio, which can then be used when it becomes necessary to develop a narrative of teaching achievement for a given purpose.

Evidence also needs to be of good quality, especially if you are seeking to make a case for the impact of your teaching in spheres of influence beyond the classroom. This is sometimes framed as seeking to answer the 'so what?' question: What difference has it made? To explore one example, you might have published a textbook in your specific discipline. Textbooks can be a valuable source of evidence about teaching achievement, as they represent the author's thinking about how a subject syllabus or curriculum might be organised. A textbook that is adopted by similar courses is clearly influencing how a subject is taught. The argument that a textbook is having such an effect would need to be supported by evidence of adoption. Book reviews and comments from staff who have adopted the book would all form part of the basket of evidence supporting a case for significant achievement. Such evidence might not be immediately forthcoming, as it takes an interval of time before a book becomes recognised as a standard text in a field. Of course, similar arguments apply to the other forms of published output, including online resources made available inside and outside the institution, perhaps under Creative Commons licences. This has been true for many years but the case for recognising such outputs has never been stronger since the start of 2020 following the pivot to teaching online during the Covid-19 pandemic and the wider use of online resources subsequently.

This issue of the quality of evidence can be framed more generically in terms of the impact that your education activities have had. The term 'impact' can have a breadth of meanings depending upon the context and can be interpreted very broadly. It might mean evidence of improvements in student outcomes or student engagement. It could refer to influences upon the practice of colleagues in your institution or beyond. It might mean evidencing contributions to learning and teaching agendas or influencing policy locally, nationally or internationally. It might refer to your contributions to team efforts of the work of project groups, committees or national bodies (Lea, 2015). A further discussion about the meaning of impact in the specific context of award applications can be found in Chapter 5.

There are many ways to approach the evidencing of teaching achievement and the approach you choose will depend partly upon the purpose for which you are gathering it (see Chapter 5).

In summary, gathering feedback about teaching achievements is an active and ongoing process involving thought and effort on the part of the person gathering that evidence, as well as exercising critical judgement on the value of any such evidence. It is in the nature of teaching that such evidence is highly diverse in form. We have given an outline of it here: the specific details will depend on your own context.

Critical questions for practice

Gathering evidence

» Are you, as a teacher, actively collecting evidence on the effectiveness of all aspects of your teaching practice?

» Do you collect evidence of your practice only at the end of a course or programme of study or also while it is still in progress?

» Do you maintain records of your teaching evidence and actively review those records on a regular basis?

» When planning your teaching activities and especially when implementing planned changes, do you build into your plans how to gather evidence about the effectiveness and impacts of your teaching?

» Do you use the teaching evidence you gather as part of formal or informal discussions of practice?

» Do you collect a range of forms of evidence, both qualitative and quantitative?

Summary

- Claims of teaching effectiveness/excellence/impact cannot be made without appropriate supporting evidence. Applications for promotion or teaching awards will usually require submission of evidence as part of your case.

- The ever-expanding range of activities that comprise teaching and education within higher education and the diverse ways in which education activities can be disseminated means that evidence of teaching achievement will be drawn from a broad range of sources.

- Unlike for research achievements, only a minority of evidence of teaching achievement will be available publicly.

- Evidence can be in the form of personal reflection from students or peers, though how appropriate it is to use this will vary from context to context (see the next chapter).

- Attention must be paid to critically evaluating the quality of evidence – including its range, value and impact – and triangulating evidence claims wherever possible.
- Evidence of teaching quality needs to be supported by a narrative that explains the nature, context and rationale of an achievement and provides evidence to verify its impact (see the next chapter).

Useful texts

Academy of Medical Sciences (2014). [online] Available at https://acmedsci.ac.uk/file-download/35943-53b159424f36e.pdf (accessed 4 August 2024).

Hillman, N and Harris, J (2019) *Recognising Teachers in the Life Sciences*. [online] Available at: https://static.physoc.org/app/uploads/2019/04/22192917/Recognising-Teachers-in-the-Life-Sciences.pdf (accessed 5 August 2024).

While these two sources deal mainly with academic careers in the biomedical disciplines, they contain much which is of broader interest to many other disciplines. Hillman and Harris (2019) provide 32 biographies of biomedical and medical scientists whose promotion has been largely or exclusively through their educational achievements.

Chalmers, D (2021) Building Your Career Through Teaching. In Hunt, L and Chalmers, D (eds) *University Teaching in Focus: A Learning-Centred Approach*. 2nd ed (pp 328–43). Abingdon: Routledge.

This chapter focuses on the education component of an academic career. While it will be particularly relevant for colleagues in education-focused careers, it will be of interest to all academic staff whose contract includes a teaching component. The book also contains a chapter by Trigwell on the scholarship of teaching and learning.

Debowski, S (2012) *The New Academic: A Strategic Handbook*. Maidenhead: Open University Press.

This academic career book contains a section on the teaching component of an academic career and includes a chapter on the scholarship and research of learning and teaching.

Lea, J (ed) (2015) *Enhancing Learning and Teaching in Higher Education: Engaging with the Dimensions of Practice*. Maidenhead: McGraw Hill Education, Open University Press.

A book written as a guide to help those seeking professional recognition for their roles in teaching and learning including, but not limited to, those seeking fellowship of the Higher Education Academy.

Chapter 5 | Presenting the evidence

Teaching achievements: using similar evidence to support different kinds of writing

Although the previous chapter explored the kinds of evidence you need to consider when evidencing teaching achievements, the evidence alone is not sufficient. Most of it will not 'speak for itself' and needs to be written in a way that interprets it for the intended readership. In the words of Bamber and Stefani (2016, p 8), *'rigour comes from accepting the provisionality of understanding, and from asking difficult, reflective questions around what we are evaluating and how'*. Most often, this is done through writing a narrative account of achievements.

Reasons why you may need to evidence the value of your teaching achievements include a job application or academic promotion, a submission for a teaching award and writing for professional recognition – against Advance HE's Professional Standards Framework or for SEDA's Fellowships Scheme, for example. Each of these requires a slightly different approach, and indeed requirements for promotion, awards and recognition commonly vary between themselves as well. However, although the approach and style of writing need to be adapted to each context, all require you to present your achievements as evidence against particular criteria.

Writing an academic promotion application

Promotion applications need to follow particular institutional procedures. A clear understanding of what these are and engagement with any available guidance are prerequisites for success. Generally, however, evidence for teaching is likely to include quantitative elements – such as lists of courses taught, student evaluation scores and positions of responsibility held – alongside supporting statements from senior and/or external colleagues, and your own narrative. One of the challenges is that promotion criteria were often designed with research achievements in mind, and only latterly have been tweaked to accommodate those relating to learning and teaching. Some learning and teaching promotion criteria and career pathways still retain a legacy of this in their wording and in the weighting given to particular kinds of achievements – for example, peer-reviewed pedagogical publications as a counterpart to subject-based research publications and external funding for pedagogical projects to mirror research funding (Cook-Sather et al, 2019). Such criteria are in danger of failing to accurately reflect the nature of the learning and teaching landscape, including the relative scarcity of funding and the small amounts available, certainly in comparison to some subject research areas. This also potentially weights recognition towards external markers of esteem or prestige without asking questions about positive impact internally on student learning or staff teaching practices. Furthermore, criteria which rely heavily on specific prescribed achievements are unlikely to give due credit to the full range of teaching achievements. The diverse nature of teaching contributions means that they are best rewarded through an appreciative or 'strengths-based approach' (Fung and Gordon, 2016). Given that institutional practice varies substantially, you will need to acquaint yourself with criteria thoroughly before you wish to apply – ideally a year or two before – so that you can address any gaps in practice that may prove to be barriers. Some find that even this is not long enough, as they may face a choice between engaging in work they feel is important and work that 'ticks boxes' purely for the sake of promotion. There can therefore be a benefit to thinking even further ahead, to allow for career planning that is authentic to your teaching interests and personal teaching practice through deeper critical reflection (Kreber, 2013).

To understand your own activity in these terms, in Chapter 3 we showed how it can be helpful to think about those activities through the three lenses of the scope of the activity; its sphere of influence; and the source of evidence (Advance HE, 2013c).

This model allows you to understand your overall contribution and its impact. While these criteria may not map directly to your university's promotion criteria, it can be expected that all three of these categories would look very different at different points in your career. In terms of career progression and reward expressed simply, you would expect something like the following in Table 5.1.

Table 5.1 How scope of influence and the nature of evidence may change with career progression

	Early career	**Mid-career**	**Later career**
Scope of activity	Focused on working directly with students. Starting to take on other roles.	Increasingly focused on roles and responsibilities at department/school level (eg programme leadership, admissions tutor) and possibly more widely.	Senior leadership engagement, formally and/or informally; external positions of responsibility.
Sphere of influence	Mainly internal – school/department.	School level and possibly more widely internally and externally.	Institution wide and external, including nationally and possibly internationally.
Source of evidence	Mainly students and self; some from peers.	Typically more balanced between students, self and peers.	Mostly from peers, with a substantial amount of this coming from institution-level and/or external sources.

Between us, we, the authors, have extensive experience of mentoring applicants for different kinds of professional recognition, including promotion and awards. Common errors we have encountered when mentoring would-be promotion applicants is the false expectation that influence on their own students, and evidence drawn from their own interactions with students, will be sufficient for promotion to more senior grades. In fact, promotion to more senior grades often depends on leadership and/or external impact beyond your department or university, including publications of some kind (Cook-Sather et al, 2019; Fung and Gordon, 2016).

Universities differ in their precise requirements for promotion applications, with some requiring them to be written in a reflective way and others being more like a job application in style, with the process geared towards showing your achievements in the best possible light against the criteria. In the US, a teaching portfolio is often required for tenure-track confirmation. However, whatever your institution's approach, reflection does play a role and we will explore this below.

Example 5.1

Case study: Professor Nicola King

Professor Nicola King is Associate Pro-Vice Chancellor for Education in the Faculty of Environment, Science and Economy at Exeter University, UK.

Within her institution, she has contributed to a number of cross-university groups and committees and is a leader in interdisciplinary science education. She was part of a small team who set up an interdisciplinary Natural Science undergraduate programme open to students with only one science subject plus maths at A level – thus removing barriers to certain groups of students. This new programme saw students with a single science A level achieving equal levels of attainment to those with qualifications more traditional for entry to a science degree. There was also a better gender balance (50–50) than on other physical science programmes at the university. She is now further developing this widening participation agenda by leading the development of foundation programmes, including Natural Sciences with a Foundation Year.

As part of facilitating this success, she developed a pastoral tutoring framework – featuring resources, training and guidance for academic staff – which has led to the highest NSS scores in the university and other increased student satisfaction data. This has led to her influencing institution wide as a member of the Senior Tutor Forum.

She has collaborated internally, externally and with students to create and embed a range of innovative digital learning resources, including virtual lab simulation tools.

In 2019 she was elected inaugural Chair of the Society for Natural Science, an organisation supporting interdisciplinary education and research in the sciences; she has guided the Society to the point where it has a national voice and informs policy. Under her leadership, the Society has developed an accreditation framework, which has supported 15 institutions to date to review provision to provide support for students to develop the skills to study sciences in a genuinely interdisciplinary manner, rather than as individual subjects side by side. She was awarded Principal Fellow of the Higher Education Academy in 2021 and a National Teaching Fellowship in 2022, just after being promoted to professor.

Professional recognition

Professional recognition is a way of validating your existing experience. There are a number of schemes which do this for learning and teaching in universities. In the UK these include the Professional Standards Framework (PSF), the Fellowships Scheme of the Staff and Educational Development Association (SEDA), and the CMALT accreditation framework of the Association for Learning Technology (ALT). The PSF was launched in 2006 in the UK, originally for UK university staff. It has since been revised twice, with a major sector-led review in 2022 and the launch of a revised PSF in 2023. Advance HE is the custodian of the scheme. Over this time, use of the PSF has grown rapidly across 90 countries. At the time of writing, the number of staff who had gained recognition of their teaching practice against one of the framework's four Descriptors was nearing 187,000. The PSF is a framework which higher education institutions can use to develop their own provision, subject to successful accreditation by Advance HE, leading to the award of one of the four categories of Fellowship. For many institutions it is also often a key performance indicator (KPI) of the professional standing of its staff engaged in teaching. In contrast to promotion and other teaching awards, PSF recognition is more geared towards demonstrating evidence of effective practice. An important advantage is that it is criterion based rather than competitive. Thus, unlike the promotion context, it is appropriate to explore instances where practices of teaching or supporting learning did not go to plan; how the learning from that was used; how practice has developed over time; and the impact of ongoing CPDL and scholarship.

Professional recognition processes raise the profile of learning and teaching and are tools for development and change. How well this works depends to an extent on how institutions and individuals choose to engage with them, as a brief look at some of the literature surrounding the example of the PSF reveals. Many individuals approach professional recognition wholly or partly from an intrinsic desire to develop their professionalism, even where it is required for probation, appraisal or promotion. However, others approach it reluctantly and purely instrumentally, where the meeting of these institutional requirements is the goal rather than a developmental objective, as Peat (2015) has noted in relation to the PSF. This can raises challenges for its effectiveness (Spowart and Turner, 2020). In an institutional context, how a recognition framework is framed and supported, through senior staff validation, mentorship structures, workload allocation or its absence, and the way in which achievement is celebrated, all contribute to staff attitudes and perceptions. As an example of the complexity of this, Smart et al (2021) explore the potential effectiveness and benefits of institutions adopting a dialogic assessment format for those seeking fellowship recognition via their university's provision. They note that how this is designed and supported by the institution is critical to ensuring the applicant's experience is based on developmental values: *'enabling of voice, valuing of the person, respectful of practice'* (Smart et al, 2021, p 41). The value of the PSF and similar frameworks thus depends on how the process of gaining recognition is approached at an individual level, and how they are deployed and supported at an institutional one. Botham's (2015) study of an accredited CPD framework is one example of where participation was found to benefit individuals and their departments. The same study also rightly points to the need for further research in this complex area.

Teaching awards

Teaching awards cover a huge range of possibilities, including internal or external recognition. They can be awarded for a particular achievement or general contribution to the university, sector or discipline, and they can be student, peer or self-nominated.

Institutional teaching award schemes for staff in higher and tertiary education are in place in many countries and more continue to be established. In the UK and internationally, many universities have award schemes run by the institution designed to reward individuals and, in some cases, teaching teams, on a competitive basis (Chan and Chen, 2023; Lubicz-Nawrocka and Bunting, 2019). Many universities now also have fully student-led teaching awards (Edinburgh University Students' Association, 2016; Kara and Barton, 2023; Thompson and Zaitseva, 2012).

National teaching award schemes include the Canadian 3M scheme, which is the longest-established scheme of its kind. It was established by the Society for Teaching and Learning in Higher Education (STLHE), with up to ten awards being made in any one year (Society for Teaching and Learning in Higher Education, 2021). In the UK the National Teaching Fellowship Scheme (NTFS) was established in 2000 as a recommendation of the *Higher Education in the Learning Society: Main Report* (The Dearing Report, 1997). More details about the criteria for the NTFS are provided in Example 2.1 in Chapter 2. Initially there was a £50,000 award to enable the recipients to develop teaching enhancement projects. That this is no longer the case reflects a wider decline in grants and awards for teaching. All higher education providers in the UK who are members of Advance HE are eligible to enter up to three staff, with 55 awards being made annually (Skelton, 2004, 2005; Ashwin, 2021).

Like promotion applications, these teaching awards are usually an opportunity to demonstrate achievements against criteria, but often they also invite applicants to reflect in depth upon those achievements. Applicants are asked to demonstrate reach, value and impact. For example, when thinking about the reach of an activity, it might be relevant to demonstrate an understanding that effective pedagogies are inclusive and take account of the needs of a wide range of learners. Additionally, effective pedagogies depend upon teacher behaviours, hence the importance of sharing good practice (Husbands and Pearce, 2012). In respect of adding value to a teaching activity, then demonstrating an awareness of the importance of quality of instruction, for example through scaffolding, would be of relevance (Coe et al, 2014). In terms of impact, education leaders should seek to '*make a credible narrative ... providing evidence of significant leadership contribution and showing how the work has made a strategic impact upon the particular context in which s/he works*' (Fung and Gordon, 2016, p 9).

In 2016, in recognition of the fact that it is not just individuals but also teams that have impacts in higher education, Advance HE introduced the Collaborative Award for Teaching Excellence (CATE) scheme to recognise and reward collaborative work. This scheme aims to recognise the work of teams in universities, consisting of up to 15 individuals, that have had demonstrable impacts upon learning and teaching in higher education (Advance HE, 2024).

Critical issues

The value of teaching award schemes

Teaching award schemes, whether institutional, led by students or awarded through national or international competition, have as their main purpose the recognition and reward of individual higher education staff (academic or professional) for excellence in their contributions to learning and teaching (Skelton, 2004, 2005; Fitzpatrick and Moore, 2015). They have been viewed as a means to promote parity of esteem between teaching and research through providing opportunities to reward teachers alongside already existing reward schemes for researchers. They have also been posited to enhance teaching excellence. However, Ashwin (2020, 2021) criticises this exemplar model of enhancement on the ground that it is based upon a flawed model of change, a contagion model, in which higher education staff identified through this form of recognition will encourage the development of teaching excellence among their colleagues. Fanghanel (2012) makes a similar criticism of this model in a different context, that of institutional learning and teaching development schemes, suggesting that *'a contamination conception of change fails to take account of the agentic responses of individual staff* (p 35).

If this contested view of the value of teaching award schemes is accepted, then what are their benefits? Skelton (2004, 2005) argues that the new professional identity that is conferred on staff who are successful in achieving an award positions them as leaders in their educational field as teachers and developers. One might argue that this is an equivalent position of status in education as would be conferred upon somebody in receipt of a national or international research fellowship. In a report for the Higher Education Academy on the National Teaching Fellowship Scheme (NTFS) Rickinson et al (2012) make a similar point, identifying that for many the award of Fellowship facilitated career progression, but noting at the same time that this could depend upon the value placed upon teaching and learning by the institution. This same report does identify the fact that impacts upon students, colleagues and institutions were more mixed, reinforcing the point made by Ashwin (2020) above. A more recent study for the Office for Students (Austen et al, 2018) notes that the study respondents felt that the scheme enhanced the status of learning and teaching and commended the NTFS as a national measure of teaching excellence. Rickinson et al (2012, p 27) do identify disadvantages of the NTFS, with the principal ones being institutions not engaging with scheme as it was felt that some National Teaching Fellows were *'not permitted to make as much contribution as they would wish'* and that institutions *'don't know what to do with their Fellows'*.

A key disadvantage of award schemes such as these is that their competitive nature means that there will be losers as well as winners. Consequently, the impact can be dysfunctional for unsuccessful applicants (Seppala and Smith, 2019).

Award schemes are clearly beneficial to many award holders, but if the full benefits of achieving an award are to be felt, it may be that award holders need to be more proactive as change agents in their institutions.

Key issues in presenting evidence

The importance of narrative: motivation, activity, impact

Whatever your achievements in learning and teaching, and whatever the reason for presenting them, there is a limit to what you can demonstrate without writing a continuous narrative. This usually means a written account but is true even in dialogic processes. For example, while a bullet-pointed list or chronological account can provide concise headlines, or an overview of achievements, it is not enough on its own to explain the reason or motivation behind an action: how and why you chose to conduct that action in a particular way; and what impact these actions had.

What did you do?

This is the foundation of your application. Without a clear narrative explanation of what you did, it is very hard to talk meaningfully about the benefits, reach, value and impact. Explaining what you did may sound straightforward, but many applications suffer from imprecision. An example might be: *'I redeveloped a programme'*. This may appear self-explanatory to the writer, but it raises a few questions. Firstly, what was your contribution to redeveloping the programme? Was it done singlehandedly, did you lead a team to do it, or were you one member of the team involved? If so, what was your role and what did you accomplish? Secondly, what was the nature of the work? What were its different stages? A lack of clarity and detail makes it easy for complex achievements to be under-appreciated. This leads quickly into the next question.

Why did you do it?

To help your readers understand what you have done, it is usually necessary to supply some context and background to what you did. You need to be able to explain why it was important to do the work you have described. What were the motivating factors? These could be to do with implementing policy and strategy. If so, it is useful to make this clear, but also to explain the purpose of the policy or strategy and what it was trying to achieve. It may be that you noticed the need for change and responded. If so, it should be clear to the reader:

- » why you felt change was needed;
- » what indicators/evidence there were that pointed in this direction;
- » the logical link between that need and any actions you then took.

Identifying the values and other considerations which affect what you choose to do and how you go about it can give deeper insights into your practice, which make your contributions clearer.

What was the impact?

Doing both of the above effectively is essential groundwork for demonstrating impact – the 'so what?'. A good question with which to begin your thinking about this is: What difference has my work made to learning and teaching? In terms of personal teaching practice, the impact may be quite immediate, such as a redeveloped module that leads to improved student feedback, learning and attainment. This can be supported by peer evidence, such as that from peer review, and external evidence, such as a statement from your programme's external examiner. More strategic work may rely on more complex combinations of evidence, akin to attempting to answer a kind of research question about your teaching (ie *'What evidence is there that this project or initiative achieved its intended goal?'*).

We said above that award and promotion applications may not require reflective writing (although universities differ on this). However, writing a successful application of any kind is likely to be built on a reflective process that involves engaging with questions such as the following.

1. Why did I do this work?
2. Why do I think it worked?
3. What evidence do I have?
4. What does this evidence enable me to claim about its effectiveness?
5. What are the limitations of what it tells me?

Knight (2021) has brought all these elements together in model she has termed DRIVE. In this model, applicants are encouraged to follow a multistep approach to constructing a narrative of teaching excellence. The first step consists of describing an activity and giving sufficient context to support an understanding of the activity. The second step is to provide a rationale for the activity, explaining why the activity was necessary or what problem it was trying to solve. The rationale might be supported by relevant sources from the learning and teaching literature. The third step is to state the impact of the initiative by explaining what changed for students, colleagues, the institution, the discipline or the sector, as relevant. The fourth and fifth steps are verification through evidence, thinking as broadly as possible.

Whichever model you have chosen to construct your narrative, the development of a narrative allows you to demonstrate the processes of professional decision making, whereby you make clear how you have brought *'Experience, Context and Judgement'* to bear on the available evidence in making these decisions (Bamber and Stefani, 2016, p 249). For example, it is possible to list sources of evidence, such as student feedback, feedback from an external examiner or peer review feedback. However, it is hard for a list of data to communicate the impact of your work on student learning. We need to know not just that students gave high evaluation scores, but their reasons for giving these scores. Collating and making sense of different perspectives on your achievements from students, colleagues and other sources of evidence has a developmental value in itself that can help shape your practice, as well as this and any future applications (Brookfield, 2017).

Ticking boxes or telling stories?

Writing a narrative against criteria creates a certain tension: you are at once selecting examples and elements of your practice to tell the 'story' of what you have done while 'box-ticking' against a list of requirements. However, for the reasons explored above, unless an application demands otherwise, it is usually better to structure it around defined achievements. Even where you must address criteria one at a time, finding a way of telling a 'story' – the motivation, action and impact – and, if the format allows, showing how these are linked to particular areas of interest, can be a helpful approach. Within your narrative, it may then be appropriate to signpost – for example, in brackets – which criterion or criteria each part of that narrative addresses.

Learning and teaching is a complex activity, and an approach that facilitates learning in one context may be ineffective or inappropriate in another. Therefore, *'evidencing value means systematically working out what our effects are, with a mix of evidence, informed by judgement'* (Bamber, 2013, p 13). The value of teaching may take considerable time to register – for example, when students leave university. As a result, evidence of effective or excellent learning and teaching tends to look very different from evidence of effective or excellent research, for which external calibration is often inbuilt in the form of journal and publisher peer-review processes, and data on citations.

The idea of value is also important in shaping a narrative. Making a claim that the work you did was effective and important carries with it an implicit statement of professional values. This is a particularly significant point if your claim of impact is being read – as is often the case – by people from beyond your immediate academic discipline or subject area. For example, there may be conventions to listing the order of authors on a paper within your discipline, which show who led the project. This may not translate to other disciplines, and you may have to make your leadership explicit. The importance of particular aspects of pedagogy, or approaches to learning, teaching and assessment, can also be highly contextual. It is often helpful to ask yourself, '*Why is this important?*' and to test your draft narrative on someone from outside your field,

Application word limits also necessitate striking a balance between demonstrating the scope or extent of achievements and the detail of those which most strongly demonstrate the impact or value. Selecting key achievements to form the centrepiece of the narrative is therefore another critical factor in ensuring that your full impact is transparent to readers. Giving undue focus to relatively minor achievements is an easy pitfall. Another is foregrounding achievements which are not the most relevant to the particular criteria.

Developing an application

Bearing these complexities in mind, many people find it challenging to present their evidence in a way that demonstrates their achievements to maximum effectiveness. This is one reason why the process of writing, for whatever kind of recognition, needs to begin in plenty of time. This allows for drafting and redrafting and seeking feedback. Even better, thinking about what we have achieved can be part of an authentic and ongoing developmental process that we engage with every year. Recognising the extent of what we have achieved as higher education teachers improves our confidence, and reflecting on these achievements can highlight the potential for important new areas of work. The reflection that comes from working to recognise our own achievements can be important in our own development, and in improving our practice as teachers and leaders in higher education. It can help us in identifying the unifying theme, or themes, in our educational work and what we bring to it that is unique. Being able to draw this theme out in the narrative allows individuals to demonstrate their values, and potentially illustrate greater impact as a result.

Often people only begin thinking about writing their promotion application in the 6 to 12 months before it is to be submitted. This can lead to a belated recognition of missed opportunities in terms of both career management and gathering evidence of impact. Annual appraisal can have an important role in supporting this. It is never too early in your career to start thinking about this and to engage with universities' promotion briefings and other support to ensure you have an adequate understanding of the process and requirements. One benefit of this is that it can highlight strengths and weaknesses at an early enough stage for them to be actionable. For example, it is not uncommon for committed university teachers to struggle to find time to disseminate their work through conferences and publications of different kinds. An early appreciation of the importance of this to gaining promotion can help focus energy on reprioritising this work, identifying opportunities for collaboration and/or approaching curriculum innovation projects with data collection and dissemination in mind from the outset.

This can mean that valuable opportunities to gather evidence of impact have been lost. Students and colleagues move on, which means it may be impossible to gather feedback or locate school or departmental data that supports your narrative of effectiveness. For example, evidence on the effect on student learning of a curriculum innovation may include student feedback and feedback from an external examiner. However, standard processes for gathering these cannot be depended upon to provide feedback specific enough to meet the applicant's needs. It may be necessary to conduct a short, separate survey of students – one or two questions may be enough. This can be done in person via a sticky note or electronically using Microsoft Forms or SurveyMonkey. It can be helpful to take five minutes of class time to do this, as part of evaluating the effectiveness of your approach which may lead to subsequent changes to practice.

Critical issues

Promotion: interpreting criteria and when to apply

Promotion criteria are written down in policy, but aspects of their interpretation can be highly contextual, and may not be interpreted consistently across the institution (see 'Critical issues' in Chapter 7). To be successful, promotion applicants need the best understanding possible of how the criteria are applied in their context, and in relation to their specific career path and achievements. As well as exploring the documentation, this is likely to involve attending university promotion briefings, which can be an opportunity to ask questions. Particularly where applicants feel their area of work is not obviously represented by the criteria, they will need opportunities to discuss this with colleagues in human resources or those elsewhere with responsibility for the promotion system or decision-making process.

There may also be times in a career when someone is particularly well positioned to demonstrate they meet particular promotion criteria. For example, if they have recently contributed a major project or have pedagogical publications which are in press, they may have a more persuasive case once there has been sufficient time for these to have an impact. Equally, institutional promotion criteria sometimes discount work conducted before the previous promotion or appointment to the role, depending on which was later. An ideally timed application in a system such as this is one in which evidence of achievement does not greatly exceed the minimum requirement, so that any further achievement can count towards future promotions.

Stage 1: Pre-writing and planning

Although people sometimes begin by launching straight into writing a draft, this can lead to time-consuming work later when it needs to be rewritten. We have established that writing for recognition or promotion involves providing evidence against criteria of some kind in a limited number of words. Planning the writing can avoid mistakes such as missing out key achievements, giving insufficient space to important work or using up valuable words by over-evidencing particular things.

While the drafting process is certainly about getting words on the page, it is also about clarifying your thoughts on what your key achievements are, what evidence of impact might look like, what evidence you already have, and what you might need to locate or begin to gather. Therefore, part of the drafting process might involve 'pre-writing' stages (Murray, 2015). This can mean notetaking, mind-mapping, informal discussion with a colleague, or audio recording your own reflections and thoughts on your key achievements. For many people, talking about their achievements is easier than writing, and a better starting point.

The purpose of this stage is to map out all the things you could include in your application. It is better to be comprehensive at this stage: selecting things for inclusion or exclusion can be done later.

Once you have a list, map or other complete record of your achievements, you can start to think about them more deeply. Three important questions to ask yourself at this point are:

1. What motivated me to do each of these activities? (the 'why')
2. What exactly did I do? If I worked in a team, what was my role? If I influenced others to act, what happened because of my leadership? (the 'what')
3. What was the result or impact? (the 'so what?')

Some of your answers to each of these three questions may be new questions at this stage. For example, you may wish to get your colleagues' perspectives about your contribution. You may note down your ideas about kinds of evidence you have; kinds you can look for; and whether any new evidence needs to be gathered. You could start by listing your achievements, and their impacts, chronologically.

Stage 2: Drafting

The first writing you do is often most valuable if it is seen as a step in a process rather than a 'draft' which simply needs revising. Having a piece of writing to critique and develop can be invaluable step in the process, particularly if you are willing to accept that much of it may look very different by the end.

Writing for recognition or promotion requires a completely different approach to academic writing. In some respects, the strategies we need to use for it are the opposite to conventions of academic writing, which usually attempt to avoid formulations which emphasise the author's subjectivity. If you want others to understand your teaching achievements, however, you need to be completely clear that you were the person who did them. This means the following.

» Writing in the first person, using 'I'.

» Using active constructions rather than passive ones, such as '**I led** the project' rather than 'the project **was conducted**'; '**I produced** a set of resources' rather than 'a set of resources **was produced**'.

» Avoiding 'we'. If you say '**we** designed and developed a new programme', for example, the extent of your role in this is unclear. This does not mean claiming others' work as your own. It simply means articulating the extent and limits of your contribution. Did you lead a team or have a particular role in the programme development? Was it your idea, and did you establish there was a market for it? It can be useful to talk to colleagues if you are unsure of their perceptions. It is particularly important to do this if more than one of you are applying for promotion or an award at the same time.

» Using verbs that do justice to your contribution. In the authors' experiences, some of the commonly used verbs which tend to underplay people's contributions are 'liaised with' or 'ensured that'. In our experience of reviewing applicants' drafts, querying what is meant by vague verbs like this often reveals a significant and skilful leadership contribution, including gaining buy-in from colleagues, students or other stakeholders. Some verbs you might find useful instead are 'lead', 'manage', 'mentor', 'co-ordinate', 'influence', 'initiate' or 'project manage'.

» Once you have a full draft, you may need to check again that the following are clear:

- motivation (the why);
- action (the what);
- impact (the 'so what').

For promotion and teaching awards, the writing tone required might be descriptive rather than reflective in focus – more akin to a job application (this varies between promotion schemes). However, because effective descriptive writing against criteria still involves articulating reasons for action, selecting the best examples to highlight and identifying the evidence of impact, a reflective process is still needed.

Critical questions for practice

» Do you routinely collect and curate evidence of your teaching achievements?

» Do you make time to engage with your colleagues in informal conversations about your teaching?

» When preparing an application, whether for promotion, an internal or external teaching award or for professional recognition, do you look at the criteria well in advance of the application being made?

» In preparing an application, do you seek support from colleagues who have recently been successful, whether in your discipline or an unrelated discipline, perhaps by discussing the process with them or asking to see their successful application?

Summary

- Although only some contexts and criteria require you to write reflectively, there is a reflective *thought process* involved whenever you are writing for reward and recognition. This is because of the need to think critically about your achievements and make claims about them that are defensible.

- Because education-related achievements are contextual, writing about them needs to draw on different kinds of evidence. Therefore, a strong narrative tends to be needed to demonstrate impact and effectiveness.

- Narratives of evidence need to be balanced to give most space to those achievements which best demonstrate impact in relation to the particular criteria. If they are to be fully understandable, narratives also need to be situated within the context of the institutions and the settings in which they were undertaken, and these contexts need to be clearly and concisely explained.

- Because of the complexity of writing an account of your practice against criteria, with supporting evidence, planning and drafting are important stages.

Useful texts

Advance HE (2013c) *Making Evidence Count.* [online] Available at: www.advance-he.ac.uk/knowledge-hub/promoting-teaching-making-evidence-count (accessed 20 June 2024).

Promoting Teaching was a Higher Education Academy funded project aimed at guiding and improving academic promotion policies and practice for recognising and rewarding teaching. Making Evidence Count *was one output from the project focusing on the evidencing of teaching achievement.*

Fung, D and Gordon, T (2016). *Rewarding Education and Education Leaders.* [online] Available at: www.advance-he.ac.uk/knowledge-hub/rewarding-educators-and-education-leaders (accessed 20 June 2024).

A report for Advance HE discussing the importance of teaching leadership and its reward in research-intensive institutions.

Chapter 6 | Support for applicants

Why should institutions establish award and promotion applicant support?

In this chapter, we explore the benefits of offering institutional support to applicants, in relation to promotion and award applications. It is likely to be of interest to those in institutions looking to set up provision to support an increased number of successful awards or promotion applications in relation to learning and teaching. This can in turn build up leadership capacity. Some of the discussion is also likely to be helpful to individuals looking to establish an individual or informal mentoring or coaching arrangement, enabling them to better understand what kinds of support could help them. Support can demystify application processes and encourage applicants to think rigorously about their evidence, improving success rates and supporting the development of (future) leaders of learning and teaching. Some of what we say draws on our professional learning from designing, developing and delivering approaches to provide support in institutional contexts.

As we have explored, gaining personal reward and recognition for achievements in learning and teaching can involve overcoming several barriers. These combine to make a powerful case for the importance of mentoring applicants for promotion, recognition and awards. In Chapter 2 we explored the contested nature of teaching excellence. This makes it important for applicants to understand how it is interpreted in the context of a particular award or promotion scheme (see also Chapter 5). Chapter 4 explored the complex nature of identifying, gathering and presenting evidence. The privileged status enjoyed by research over teaching adds a further layer of complexity (see Chapters 1 and 2). Blackmore (2016) distinguishes between the 'prestige' accrued by researchers and the 'reputation' developed by those with achievements in education. One of the results of this privileging of research over teaching is that individual staff may begin measuring themselves against an ideal – 'the hegemonic academic' – which refers to a set of commonly internalised career expectations which are closely tied to research prestige (Wren Butler, 2021). Wren Butler found imposter syndrome of this kind to be prevalent at all levels of academia. The cultural privileging of research means that annual appraisal conversations may not address learning and teaching contributions fully – or indeed at all – which removes an element of support and career development. In addition, structural biases mean that minoritised groups are less successful in achieving promotion. For all these reasons, staff need support to effectively evidence their achievements in learning and teaching.

What are the considerations in setting up institutional support for applicants?

» **Who is best placed to offer support**? Support that meets institutional and individual needs requires the involvement of people with a firm understanding of the recognition and reward processes they are supporting. This enables them to advise authoritatively.

» **What experience are they likely to have?** It can send a powerful message to applicants if those involved in mentoring or coaching applicants have personal experience of successfully applying for awards or promotion. However, someone who has been successful may only have their own experience to draw upon, which is a potential risk and limitation. Staff would be best placed if they have had experience of seeing a range of successful, and unsuccessful, applications. There may be other academic and professional services staff, such as educational developers with a role in supporting reward and recognition who can bring this to the table. Colleagues in human resources may need to be involved in an advisory capacity. It may be worthwhile to nurture a small group of (future) leaders in learning and teaching towards their own promotions as a first step to growing a pool of coaches, facilitators or mentors. Alternatively, an external coach or consultant with appropriate background is an option if budget allows.

» **What are the boundaries and limitations of support?** The boundaries of any support offered should be clearly set. The application needs to be the applicant's own work. Institutions will need to consider and define what is reasonable support with writing, and what is an inappropriate level of guidance. It should be clear that support and guidance are advisory only and not a guarantee of success.

» **At what stage of an application should support take place?** If the timing of mentoring opportunities is too close to deadlines for promotion or awards, this may give an unintended signal that the mentor is to be heavily involved in the final submission, including proofreading. It may also lead to their input being seen as instruction and direction rather than support or facilitation. This may ultimately be detrimental to the final application. We have found six to eight months ahead of a promotion or an award deadline to be helpful timing, allowing time to guide the applicant in their own process of evidence gathering and writing, rather than getting drawn into the detail of the application.

There are a range of different approaches to consider. Peer mentoring has also been shown to be effective in supporting career development and progression (Mayer et al, 2014; Ockene et al, 2017). It may be appropriate, with permission and suitable observation of confidentiality, to facilitate this by putting mentees in contact. Zambrana et al (2015) identify a lack of mentors who understand the specific challenges from minoritised perspectives as a barrier to career development. Institutions should explore approaches to address this which serve to give staff from minoritised groups within higher education or within their field an institutional 'voice' (Bhopal, 2020).

Finally, the Spectrum Approach to mentoring is a model developed in response to the lack of evidence-based approaches in the literature to mentoring specifically for academics (Harvey et al, 2017). This approach, supported by online resources and a viewable register of mentors, encourages staff to focus on a particular goal and consider which people can best help them to reach it. Instead of focusing solely on mentoring as a one-to-one relationship, it supports people to draw on a range of different mentoring relationships. These may be internal or external to the institution and may include group as well as individual mentoring. Framing mentoring in this way has potential benefits for promotion applicants in learning and teaching, who may not have a single obvious role model who has followed a similar path. Group workshops are also a possibility if they can offer the space for applicants to try out ideas and receive feedback from facilitators or peers.

Example 6.1

Institutional case study: blending individual and group support

At Newcastle University, the authors and colleagues established a programme of support for promotion applicants. This included the following.

» Two workshops: one on evidence gathering and another on building a narrative. Participants were free to attend either or both of these.

» Individual coaching sessions. Attendance at any of these was entirely voluntary, and there was no obligation for participants to have also attended the workshops.

The flexibility and choice available to participants were seen as important to enable people with different roles and commitments to benefit. Feedback from participants, particularly those attending one-to-one coaching sessions, mentioned a range of ways in which the session had clarified their understanding or things they would do differently as a result. These included approaches to both collecting and presenting evidence.

These activities were supported by a key document which laid out possible sources of evidence for each grade of promotion. This document was designed to be used by all involved in promotion based on learning and teaching, including applicants and promotion committees. The aim was to improve the shared institutional understanding of the criteria.

This document was accessible from a web page, which also housed links to further resources for applicants. These included short case studies based on recent, successful promotion applications; short videos of successful promotion applicants talking about the process of application; and an annotated application statement, highlighting strengths and weaknesses.

What encourages participants to take up support?

Once any programme of support is established, it needs to be publicised to attract the staff who are likely to benefit – those thinking about promotion in the short term or planning ahead. This is not easy: those engaging most readily are likely to be from privileged groups. It may be harder to attract women or non-binary staff, and staff of colour. Attempts to address this can easily become procedural or performative rather than effecting significant change (see eg Bhopal, 2020). There may therefore need to be some work to proactively identify staff. One route to this can be inviting key individuals in strategic positions – for example, school directors of learning and teaching. A second part of this can be inviting these individuals to suggest other staff who may be interested in, and benefit from, support. A third approach involves spreading the message more widely – for example, through online communities, email lists, at school meetings, and through internal learning and teaching development networks – to get out an inclusive message which makes it clear that this support is for everyone, including those without immediate plans to apply.

It is helpful when staff do access support a long way in advance: promotions in particular are not based on the kind of achievements that are accomplished overnight, and it's useful for staff to plan their careers with the necessary breadth of academic activity in mind. This can avoid long-term disillusionment and loss of morale. It is also an important message as it makes signing up for support of this kind seem less presumptuous – something that is likely to make it less intimidating. This makes it more likely that staff from under-represented groups, or who lack confidence, or who are simply unaware of how promotable they already are, will attend.

Critical issues

Structural inequities

Structural inequities have a significant impact upon career progression, including that of female and racially minoritised staff (Shepherd, 2017; Bhopal, 2020). Bhopal (2020) points to the need for universities to operate strategically and proactively to address this and for Black and ethnic minority staff to have a voice which enables them to influence within university structures, for example through an equality, diversity and inclusion committee. Mentoring itself, however, cannot address societal problems. An idea of mentoring as something which can 'fix' this by addressing a deficit in the individual should be resisted (Shepherd, 2017).

Unlike traditional mentoring, sponsorship mentoring has been shown to reduce opportunity gaps for minoritised groups (Munir, 2022). In sponsorship mentoring, the mentor goes beyond an advisory role to become an advocate for the mentee in an institutional or broader context. For example, they may put the mentee forward as a possible candidate for internal promotion and secondment opportunities. Thus, it is the institution that is acknowledged as deficient, and the mentor takes steps to address this for their mentee.

Mentoring presents opportunities for institutional learning. Ideally, there should be a diverse pool of mentors, with whom the mentors feel able to discuss their career ambitions and frustrations and share concerns about discrimination.

What is the focus of support for award and promotion applicants?

Applicants often appreciate a focus on identifying the most important of their achievements and the full scope of their relevant activity. This has to be tailored to the context of the particular award or promotion criteria or framework. It may in addition be appropriate to outline future plans and think in terms of how the award or promotion might support these. However, reward and recognition are usually given based on evidence of impact to date. The focus of support is often therefore on looking backwards more than it does forwards. It supports the applicant to ask themselves the following questions.

- » What have I done?
- » What evidence of impact do I have?
- » What other evidence of past achievements might I need to gather?
- » Have I done enough to make me competitive for the award/promotion in question?

Broadly speaking, it's only if the answer to the final question is 'no' that the conversation starts to look to the future, to address questions such as the following.

- » What other steps could I take to make myself competitive? Are there specific areas of experience or achievement I need to demonstrate?
- » Which of these are most congruent with my interests, strengths, existing plans and scope for action?
- » Over what timescale can I achieve these new objectives?

While the kind of support we're discussing here has clear and focused goals, it may be appropriate to widen this focus to encompass wider contextual issues if that emerges as a key issue for a group of individual.

How do you structure support for awards or promotion?

As earlier chapters highlight, criteria for awards and promotions differ, depending on the purpose and the institution. These criteria certainly need to be in the mind of any potential applicant to ensure they keep their efforts on track. However, beginning a workshop or coaching or mentoring conversation with a deep focus on criteria can be counter-productive for several reasons:

- » it can lead to a 'tick-box' approach;
- » it can reduce the scope for exploring the complexity of the individual's achievements when one achievement addresses two or more of the criteria;
- » the language of criteria (eg 'strategic leadership') may exacerbate anxiety and reduce confidence if the individual hasn't yet developed a strong sense of their own impact.

It is often easier to work on such applications if reflection on achievements and future career plans is already an established habit. Where staff are ready to focus on criteria straightaway, it is often because previous attempts or similar applications mean they have already done the groundwork. For many others, there are one or two preceding steps (see Chapters 3 and 4).

Questions for early on can usefully uncover who the individual is and how they see themselves, professionally speaking, and might include the following.

» What are you particularly proud of?
» What drives or motivates you in your work? (Why do you do it?)
» What do you hope your students and/or colleagues would say about you?
» What is distinctive about what you bring to your work?

These can be helpful to the applicant in establishing, or reminding themselves of, their values, motivations and other factors in their professional identity. They also provide whoever is supporting them with insights to inform the development of the application.

The 'identity' questions discussed above form a useful foundation for identifying achievements and impact. Some 'headline' achievements may emerge from them. Starting by discussing those achievements which are most substantial, or most important to the applicant, is usually a constructive way to build confidence.

Once they have seen how they can make a case for impact using one or more of these, they can start to develop a narrative of impact. Mentoring conversations can usefully work from the past up to the present through a reflective process.

Questions to prompt this might include the following.

» What was achieved?
» What was its purpose or motivation? (Why was it done?)
» What was your role?
» If collaborative, how is this distinct from others' roles on the project?
» What wouldn't have happened if you hadn't been involved?
» Has it made an impact/brought about change?
» What evidence do you have for this?
» What further evidence could you gather?

Examples of evidence of teaching achievements provide a frame of reference for a conversation by holding a mirror up to practice. Chapter 4 is potentially a useful resource here to shape activities and discussions.

The conversation can then move to evaluating achievements against the promotion criteria. Useful questions here might be the following.

» What is your biggest achievement? Which one or more criteria do you think it addresses?

» Where do your other achievements map to?

» Are there any weak areas or gaps?

What problems occur in the mentoring and support of applicants?

Difficulties with writing

While for many the mentoring process is helpful and the application relatively straightforward, for others it can present difficulties. Colleagues from numerate or STEM disciplines, or from higher education professions which do not involve much narrative writing, sometimes experience a barrier due to this lack of background or practice. Those from an arts, humanities or social sciences background often find it easier, as they are more likely to be skilled in creating and shaping narratives for particular purposes. For those colleagues for whom writing in this style does not feel natural, it is often helpful to plan writing carefully, starting with discussion before putting pen to paper. For many, experienced writers or not, the act of writing about themselves can be inhibiting and feel exposing. Informal discussion is often a better starting point to help identify key achievements before moving on to developing a full list of them and developing the narrative around them, as described in earlier chapters – demonstrating what was done, why it was important and what the impact or outcome was. In the authors' experience, most mentees, regardless of prior experience of writing, benefit from an approach which breaks the writing process down prior to constructing a full narrative. It can be helpful to recognise that writing in any style or for any purpose is in fact a learned skill and not something that comes naturally to anyone.

Critical issues

Issues in supporting reflective writing

1. Defining reflection

   People unfamiliar with the term may need to see examples of reflective writing to understand what it is. This will need breaking down for them further with reflective questions. Using questions like these can act as scaffolding to help people build up the information they need to form into a narrative. Prior to this, it is helpful to discuss the purpose of reflective writing and what it can communicate that other forms of writing cannot. Reflective writing allows us to express the multi-layered processes of professional decision making which we use every day and which are influenced by many kinds of information, including knowledge from prior experience, knowledge from the literature, advice from colleagues and peers, and knowledge of other projects.

2. Resistance to the word 'reflection'

   The word 'reflection' can sound quite woolly and unscientific, and at odds with professional and academic identities. Although professional reflection is well established across a range of fields, to some people the word may connote a kind of aimless contemplation rather than the rigorous process that critical reflection has the potential to be. In fact, in relation to learning and teaching, what critical reflection often aims to do is bring rigour and evidence to areas of work which are often done in ways that have become taken for granted.

   It can therefore be helpful to avoid 'reflection' as a term and focus instead on exploring what 'evidence of effectiveness' means in a field as complex as learning and teaching – a heavily context-dependent and relational area of work. This is something that more people are comfortable with. It may be helpful to thematise the fact that the kinds of evidence which we use to inform our professional practice are necessarily broader ranging than the evidence that we use in academic work.

3. Separating reflective processes from writing processes

   As we have seen, the process of writing is complex in itself. People self-censor and are often highly selective in choosing what to write down.

Those new to reflective writing may see quite important professional reflections as inappropriate to include in a written narrative document. For this reason, it can be helpful to begin the reflective process by addressing some of our proposed questions (see above) in dialogue. This dialogue could be with peers in an informal co-mentoring or workshop session, or in a one-to-one support setting. Voice recording to capture their initial thoughts before writing them down is another useful tool. This allows the focus to be on identifying the useful pieces of reflective information without moving too quickly to questions of how to express them in writing.

What if aspects of career progression conflict with values or identity?

Some colleagues feel that applying for reward and recognition conflicts with their personal values or identity. Looking closely at promotion criteria sometimes makes it apparent that they need to think strategically if they are to gain experience in particular areas where they currently lack it. This can be uncomfortable. Some individuals feel an acute discomfort with the idea of devoting time to activities which they do not see as priorities or are not well aligned with their own personal and professional values. This can be particularly pronounced where there is a danger that this will take them away from work – often with students – which they feel is of more obvious and direct importance. It can be helpful for mentors to explore with these individuals the personal, professional and academic values which they feel are at stake. Sometimes there may be a solution in working towards the promotion or award goal more slowly than anticipated, so they are able to build the experience they need alongside other work which is important to them. For others, it may be helpful to look ahead and consider how the promotion or reward is likely to further enable the work which they most value. As Swartzel (2021, p 1) suggests: *'Educators tend to be altruistic. They derive joy in helping others. Putting a focus on themselves may be too uncomfortable. However, as faculty move along in their careers, they realise that they are able to help others more as they themselves are rewarded'*.

Swartzel highlights just one way in which personal credibility can be hugely important in higher education when it comes to furthering agendas around learning and teaching. The authors have diverse personal experiences of working in professional services, consultancy and senior academic roles in discipline-based departments and specialist learning and teaching departments. Moving between these positions has highlighted for us quite how arbitrary perceptions of credibility and authority can be and how much status, particularly academic status, counts in enabling individuals to act as agents of change. Promotions and awards often open doors to collaborations and to new responsibilities, which are then another important source of learning. Gaining promotion, or other forms of recognition, can thus further enable individuals to participate in learning and teaching roles and projects which align with their values. Mentors, role models or staff with specific expertise may be able to talk about this from the basis of personal experience or case studies, ideally from within the applicant's institution. Sharing and discussing these may open a way forward.

How can an individual show their impact in the context of a collaborative achievement?

Many feel uncomfortable with singling out their individual achievements when so much learning and teaching work is collaborative and collegial in nature. Strategies which might help are:

- » encouraging applicants to consider what wouldn't or couldn't have happened without their involvement and ensuring their application centres this;
- » encouraging the applicant to seek feedback from supportive colleagues about how their impact is perceived;
- » emphasising that writing about their own individual contributions is not the same as devaluing those of their colleagues.
- » exploring forms of recognition which value and acknowledge the importance of collaboration – for example, the UK's Collaborative Awards for Teaching Excellence (CATE).

What if applicants struggle with time commitment?

One final reason for difficulty engaging with support is where staff are not allocating themselves enough focused time with which to achieve it. Preparing an application requires careful thought and it is not usually the kind of work that can easily be accomplished in short bursts. Given the huge and competing demands on staff time in twenty-first-century higher education, this is not to be underestimated. Berg and Seeber (2016) explore this issue, and possible ways of addressing it, in more detail in their book *The Slow Professor*. Where a member of staff seems to be struggling to develop their application it is worth discussing questions of time, including the following.

- » How long are they able to work on it at any one time? Developing a full understanding of their contributions and achievements, and turning them into an effective narrative, tends to require periods of focus beyond the odd hour here and there.

- » How frequently are they able to work on it? Leaving gaps of more than a week or two means they will find it harder to pick up where they left off, and move their thinking forward, on each occasion.

- » Are there personal strategies they can use to free up time to work on it in a more regular or focused way? Some people find that this is the ideal kind of task to complete on a train journey, for example.

- » How many other projects are they currently engaged with? They may realise that they simply do not have the headspace to dedicate to the task and need to pause work on their application. This may involve deferring it until the next opportunity. Alternatively, there may be other projects they can pause in order to prioritise their application. In this regard too, writing retreats can provide valuable space to allow this prioritisation.

If not consciously identified and addressed, any of these issues can sabotage an application. The resulting failure to submit, or an unsuccessful outcome, can be particularly demoralising to skilled and committed people who are unused to having difficulties of this kind. It can also feel exposing, as for any internal awards, or internal endorsement to pursue external ones, you will have been making your case to colleagues. Damage to morale creates further setbacks which need to be overcome.

What support can help colleagues whose promotion applications have been unsuccessful?

This leads on to the challenge of supporting those who have suffered a blow to their self-esteem through repeated lack of success. This can feel devastating to the individual concerned. It is generally constructive to establish the reasons behind this lack of success. Possible reasons are:

- » the application was not effective – for example, it didn't go into enough depth, breadth or provide sufficient evidence;

- » structural reasons in the promotion process – that is, the way the criteria are written and/or applied make it extremely difficult to get promoted based on their particular kinds of achievements;

» local issues – for example, a line manager who does not properly understand the process or support the individual;

» issues with the promotion committee, including possible changes of membership and/or inconsistencies in the way criteria are being applied.

Gathering contextual information and feedback on the application can help to minimise the tendency of the individual to internalise their initial lack of success. It is important to allow time to reflect on and learn from what happens. It may equally be helpful to agree ground rules for a particular mentoring session or a sequence of them, so that the focus is on future possibilities rather than past disappointments.

Critical questions for practice

Designing and targeting support

» What issues do staff raise about the promotion process?

» How might any of the issues raised be addressed with staff through appropriate support prior to applying?

» Are there patterns in the reasons for unsuccessful promotion applications based on educational achievements?

» Are staff applying for promotion based on their educational achievements being promoted evenly across the institution?

» Are there sufficient promoted staff to provide leadership and support where it's needed across your institution?

» Is it just applicants who need support, or is there work to be done with departmental heads and line managers, to ensure that local support for applicants is consistent with promotions policy?

Summary

- Preparing a successful award or promotion application is a more complex and difficult process than is sometimes recognised.

- An effective programme of support needs to be widely communicated to encourage participation from all staff and should be informed by an understanding of structural inequalities and barriers to progress.

- A support offer, comprising coaching, mentoring, workshops, online resources, or a combination of these, can support reward and recognition of staff for their achievements in learning and teaching, and provide supportive spaces to deal with disappointment and demoralisation where applications are unsuccessful.

- Staff offering or contributing to such support need sufficient training or experience to appreciate how to structure conversations to best support applicants and the range of their experiences.

Useful texts

Bhopal, K (2020) Gender, Ethnicity and Career Progression in Higher Education: A Case Study Analysis. *Research Papers in Education*, 35(6): 706–21.

This paper is based on interviews with female staff at an institution which had taken measures to improve diversity in promoted roles. It identifies successes and challenges and is thus a useful read for anyone seeking to establish support for those seeking promotion.

Munir, F (2022) Sponsorship Mentoring: Development Resources for Higher Education. Advance HE. [online] Available at: www.advance-he.ac.uk/knowledge-hub/sponsorship-mentoring-development-resources-higher-education-institutions (accessed 19 March 2024).

These resources give a comprehensive guide to sponsorship mentoring and its advantages, including addressing inequalities for those from under-represented groups.

Chapter 7 | Institutional perspectives on teaching evidence and some conclusions

Institutional policies

In the preceding chapters we have demonstrated the value of rigour in evidencing achievements for individuals, teaching teams and institutions and, ultimately, for the students we all teach and support.

In Chapters 1 and 2 we explored the discourses of teaching excellence and the need for institutions to make claims about excellent teaching to communicate to potential applicants for their courses, governments and national bodies, or in order to attain high placings in ranking tables. All of these need to have their bases in evidence of teaching achievements, however they are measured.

Chapters 3 and 4 set out the importance to individuals of evidencing teaching for building a career in which the main focus is education, but also those for whom teaching is a part of a mixed portfolio of activity, perhaps alongside research in their discipline(s) and with elements of leadership as well. Such evidence supports advancement through promotion, for professional recognition or awards.

Chapter 5 explored how evidence might be deployed to best effect in framing such applications. The benefits for individuals of critically reflecting upon their teaching, whatever the drivers for it, feeds into the continual development of their practice in teaching and supporting learning (Brookfield, 2017).

Mentors can play a crucial role in supporting the development of individuals, and the value of mentoring, especially but not exclusively in relation to education-focused careers, was the theme of Chapter 6.

In this concluding chapter we draw together these strands to explore evidencing teaching from an institutional perspective. What is the importance for an institution of using this evidence to recognise and reward education-focused staff and what benefits can recognition and reward of teaching bring to developing institutional agendas? What can institutions do to support their staff to develop an evidence-informed understanding of their practice and ensure that this is fairly and equitably rewarded?

The academic workforce

The structure of the academic workforce in universities has changed. The Humboldt model of a university in which both teaching and research take place has been dominant until recently and as Blackmore (2016) has explored, research has become seen as the most important indicator of institutional prestige. In this model most academic staff are expected to research but also to teach. Institutions have sought to stress to students the benefits of receiving teaching from experts in their respective fields. However, in the UK and elsewhere this picture is changing. Locke, in two reports for the Higher Education Academy (HEA) (Locke, 2014, 2016), showed that the proportion of staff with a mixed portfolio of teaching and research was declining and increasing numbers of education-focused staff were being employed. Probert (2013) has reported similar trends in Australia and in that report emphasised the importance for staff in these roles to be recognised fully by their institutions for the roles they perform. This was emphasised by Cashmore and Ramsden in their reports for the HEA (Cashmore and Ramsden, 2009a, 2009b). It is a trend that continues in the UK, with staff employed on teaching and research contracts falling to 42.5 per cent in 2021–22 (Centre for Global Higher Education, 2023; Whitchurch, 2023; Whitchurch et al, 2023).

Benefits for institutions

At the most fundamental level, it is a simple matter of equity that education-focused staff are rewarded on the basis of parity of esteem for the work they do for their institutions if they are to be motivated and retained. This is equally the case for staff for whom teaching is just a part of a portfolio that might have a predominantly research focus. Such staff should be able to feel that their teaching contribution will also be recognised alongside any other contributions they are making to the learning and agendas of their universities. This has the potential to increase staff satisfaction and retention. However, the benefits for institutions extend well beyond this. The link between reward and recognition and teaching excellence is not securely evidenced, yet at the same time it is hard to imagine fostering a culture of 'excellence' or effectiveness without teaching being recognised and rewarded.

Rewarding and recognising education-focused staff will bring several benefits to an institution through the roles they take up and the leadership they display. Often this will be in formal leadership positions, but as Brookfield (2017, p 245) emphasises, *'those with little positional authority or public profile'* can also exercise critically reflective leadership. It needs to be recognised as widely as possible by senior managers that education-focused colleagues in promoted posts will add to their institution by acting as agents of change. Such staff can be involved in mentoring, leading initiatives to develop aspects of their institution's education strategy, and linking with other universities nationally and internationally. The case studies included in this book give examples of what colleagues have achieved for the benefit of their institutions, including developing staff or leading on learning and teaching initiatives across the sector and researching aspects of practice as part of an agenda of scholarship of teaching and learning (SoTL).

In their report on SoTL, Fanghanel et al (2016) talk about SoTL providing forms of institutional capital which come about through engaging in close-to-practice research. High-quality close-to-practice research requires the robust use of research design, theory and methods to address clearly defined research questions through an iterative process of research and application (Wyse et al, 2018). Benefits to learning and teaching accrue through the critical reflection upon practice and the development of teaching, the dissemination of the work internally and externally, and the internal and external collaborations that these generate. All these activities, as well as those outlined above, will both develop learning and teaching within institutions and be of associated reputational benefit.

Institutional policies and procedures

For these benefits to be felt, institutions need to ensure that adequate plans and policies are in place to reflect a commitment to parity of esteem between teaching achievements and other achievements in reward and recognition processes. Developing shared understandings about the nature of the processes of evidencing teaching and educational achievements has a crucial role to play in demonstrating that such evidencing can be of equivalent rigour to other achievements such as research. Consequently, staff rewarded for their contributions to an education agenda can view themselves as being on a par with staff being rewarded for their research contributions. Developing such policies is not straightforward and usually will be preceded by extensive processes of consultation. Example 7.1 is taken from the HEA Promoting Teaching project and demonstrates some of the challenges involved.

One of the key issues to be faced, as outlined in Chapter 3, is that education-focused careers can be very diverse – something that is not always fully understood and reflected in institutional recognition processes. It is important therefore that promotion criteria should reflect that complexity so that this diversity is acknowledged. Something else though is required, which is the development of a shared understanding of what that diversity means. As has been demonstrated elsewhere, there is far more to an education-focused career than what happens in a classroom. This is a disciplinary issue (Becher and Trowler, 2001): those within an institution whose own expertise lies within a subject discipline rather than its pedagogy may not fully understand the discipline of education and the nature of knowledge construction within it. A lack of any single indicator of achievement or esteem, including peer-reviewed publications, funding or a particular award, should not form a barrier to promotion given the diverse ways in which dissemination can occur in education and how educational achievements can differ. Rather, individuals need to be able to build their case, drawing appropriately from a range of different achievements within a broad framework, such as the one explored in Chapter 4. The exact achievements which are recognised within a promotion scheme also need to reflect the nature of the individual institution and how far obtaining certain opportunites and associated evidence is a question of luck more than esteem or effectiveness; or indeed whether it is aligned with the nature of actual staff roles and opportunities. Where this flexibility of what evidence is recognised is not the case, it is likely that the university will face the unintended consequence of being unable to reward those who are contributing most significantly to its institutional mission in relation to student learning.

Example 7.1

The Promoting Teaching project

The overall aim of this HEA-funded project was to support higher education institutions to understand the breadth and diversity of teaching activity in higher education so that they could better frame policies and procedures in relation to teaching when promoting staff. The project built on two earlier reports for the HEA by Cashmore and Ramsden (2009a, 2009b).

The project was an international collaboration between two UK universities (Leicester and Newcastle) and two Australian universities (Wollongong and Tasmania).

One of the key outputs from the project was a series of Good Practice Benchmarks developed by staff from the four universities in collaboration to act as a resource that universities could *'employ to identify gaps and good practice in university promotion processes, decide on aspects of promotion practice to review, and refine and improve alignment between policy and practice'* (Advance HE, 2013a, p 3). The benchmarks themselves were accompanied by a Benchmarking Guide to act as a template showing universities how to

→

benchmark their promotion processes to improve the recognition of teaching (Advance HE, 2013a, 2013b).

Eighteen benchmarks were identified, grouped into six dimensions. These were:

- » Plans and policies;
- » Perceptions and practices;
- » Promotion applicants;
- » Promotion applications;
- » Promotion committee;
- » Outcomes and review.

Their aim was to support an institutional review of promotion practices that would include:

- » having in place commitments to develop policies that commit to parity of esteem between teaching and research;
- » ensuring that those policies were communicated to and supported by all staff;
- » appropriate support on evidencing teaching achievement being given to promotion applicants;
- » application forms and guidance for evidencing teaching achievement being clear and detailed;
- » promotion committees that would be appropriately balanced to represent teaching, prepared to evaluate teaching achievement and that procedures for evaluating teaching would be transparent;
- » outcomes that were sound and equitable for teaching with a cycle of review tracking recognition of teaching.

These benchmarks were developed and tested in each university through self-review. They were then reviewed across the four institutions, with advice and comments sought from an International Advisory Group. Feedback was sought from Deputy Vice Chancellors or equivalent senior management with responsibilities for teaching, learning and education.

The intention was that through such a rigorous process, academic staff could *'perceive that teaching achievements would be valued in promotion processes'* (Advance HE, 2013a, p 4).

Example 7.1 maps one route through a path to develop understanding. Such a path will start with a critical look at the statistics on promotion and the likelihood of success in applications for advancement at all grades up to full professor for differing kinds of careers. Promotion criteria are likely already to contain criteria relating to teaching. However, the following are important factors in their effectiveness.

» Regular review and revision can ensure they acknowledge the ways in which learning and teaching have changed and education-focused careers have developed.

» The value placed upon teaching needs to be clearly articulated in reward processes and relevant documentation.

» Ideally, systems need to be in place to support the gathering of teaching evidence that are validated and accepted across the institution.

» Whether criteria are modified or revised, there will need to be training for managers within schools; heads of schools; members of promotion committees, wherever they are situated in schools, faculties or at institutional level; staff in human resources departments; and, of course, the staff themselves who may be thinking of applying.

» Promotion committees will need to be appointed in ways to ensure that the diversity of careers, including education alongside other issues of diversity and equality, is recognised.

There is, though, another set of measures to be developed at the same time. Opportunities for substantive promotion need to be supported by a scaffolded approach to career development for education-focused staff. Put simply, if the promotion criteria do not align with the opportunities available and are not accessible to staff, the system will not function. Accessibility means appropriate workload considerations being addressed, as well as, for example, opportunities for educational leadership, scholarship and other development to be available in principle.

This scaffolding will start for most staff with a course in education when newly appointed. It will continue with ongoing professional development, internal funding for education projects, internal teaching award schemes and support for career building more generally, which would include support to attend and present at external events, as well as a career structure for those wishing to move into leadership. Finally, mentoring needs to be in place for staff should they wish for that level of support. These issues were dealt with more fully in Chapter 3.

The value of support and mentoring to staff and institutions

Recognition through awards, funding schemes and allocated time for educational scholarship can support staff to develop evidence-informed approaches and develop the expertise to meet the challenges of a complex and changing educational landscape. Fung and Gordon (2016, p 54) recommend that *'senior management teams (i) develop a credible and persuasive narrative regarding the importance of education to the institutional mission, in the context of competing drivers for change'* and *'use the narrative explicitly to inform and shape changes to reward and recognition processes'*. While their work focused on research-intensive institutions, the same applies to any university wishing to recognise, support and reward education-focused achievements.

In this context, there is an important role for mentoring and other forms of development to build staff capacity to contribute to institutional discussion and debate; influence practice; and facilitate positive change in learning and teaching. Given the challenges of creating a culture of parity of esteem, such mentoring support is most likely to be a vehicle for institutional change if it is fully embedded in transparent and well-supported structures for career development. For staff to be confident that their institution's commitment to learning and teaching careers is genuine, this needs to include a clear and effective pathway to promotion that recognises learning and teaching (Cashmore and Ramsden 2009a, 2009b).

Graham's (2015, 2018) study focused on engineering disciplines identifies six barriers to rewarding teaching excellence, including promotion boards' scepticism of the way teaching achievements are measured and evidenced; the difficulty of evidencing a professorial promotion case that is international in scope; and promotion boards not acting in accordance with declared policy on reward and recognition. These point to a lack of agreement in institutions about what is to be evidenced; and about why such evidence and achievements might be important and worthy of reward. Ensuring a promotion track is effective thus involves communication to ensure an institution-wide approach and understanding that is shared by promotion panels, applicants, managers and staff in human resources. As we have already discussed, this is a particular challenge given the anonymity and consequent lack of transparency around promotion applications.

Added to these challenges, Bamber (2020) points to the ways in which universities have become *'complicit'* (p 7) in the use of metrics, despite the benefits of this being small relative to their *'distorting effects on the purpose and role of universities'* (p 17) – not least in relation to education. Thus, institutional discourse and discussions of 'teaching excellence' may focus their attention at some distance from the real barriers to nurturing and rewarding committed educators. This is in addition to the heavy workloads and multiple priorities that have become defining characteristics of many staff member's experiences of working in higher education and can make it difficult for individuals to develop the educational profile they would need to support an application for promotion.

Critical issues

Confidentiality and supporting statements

Supporting statements in promotions are often an appraisal of the applicant's achievements and are generally confidential. This confidentiality – which is usual around promotion applications generally – also makes for a lack of transparency. In Sweden, in contrast to many other contexts, official records are open access. Levander et al's (2020) analysis of peer review letters supporting academic promotion in one university in Sweden found that educational contributions tended to be valued on quantity over quality, and to emphasise research achievements and PhD supervision, risking 'an uninformed and under-developed teaching profession' (p 555).

The lack of transparency in most national contexts makes it hard to monitor the implications for equality, diversity and inclusion. It is potentially very limiting to developing parity of esteem for teaching and research. Would it be more beneficial for such statements to authenticate the applicant's claims – confirming they have done what they claim – rather than to make a value judgement?

Institutional considerations in supporting applicants

Ideally, support for staff seeking reward and recognition would be at the apex of systematic support and professional conversations about teaching. Often though, this is not the case and so supporting applicants will be the beginning of such processes rather than their culmination. This can present challenges when asking staff to think deeply about their teaching practices and what they might count among its achievements. Here are some questions institutions might reflect on when establishing or reviewing the support they offer for staff engaged in learning and teaching and its leadership.

» Are teaching roles, responsibilities and achievements given their full weight in appraisal discussions, and is this supported by the accompanying documentation?

» What opportunities for career development are there for staff at different career stages – including awards, scholarship time, leadership opportunities and promotion? How do the opportunities on offer to early career staff provide the scaffolding to bigger ones later on?

» What opportunities are there for professional services and third space professionals, given their centrality to supporting and/or delivering effective learning and teaching?

» How are promotions and other successes in relation to learning and teaching shared and celebrated?

» Is mentoring and other support clearly related to opportunities for learning and teaching awards, funding, promotion and progression?

» Does the scope and quality of the support offer reflect the importance of learning and teaching to the institution, its mission and its strategic objectives?

» Is the quality and scope of support at least equal to that offered in relation to research?

» Beyond mission and policy statements, what evidence is there that engaging with the support on offer will benefit students and the careers of staff?

As well as being of intrinsic benefit to staff and the institution, this kind of infrastructure for career development is evidence of a university's level of commitment to learning and teaching. These wider questions of university culture are an essential context for our main focus on support for writing applications for awards and promotion. They help create a culture that values learning and teaching, as well as the kind of discussions that will support nuanced discussion of learning and teaching and its impact.

A well-conceived funded programme of support that aims to help applicants develop their careers over the medium term, and consequently frame a promotion application, is an important step that universities need to take if they wish to ensure teaching achievements are to be fully recognised and appropriately rewarded. Such schemes can be an important arm of policies seeking parity of esteem between teaching and other achievements. Universities wishing to improve the number of promotions for learning and teaching, or the number and quality of internal or external teaching award applications, would benefit from considering support such as mentoring, coaching, workshops and opportunities for discussion and networking in relation to learning and teaching clearly targeted at staff with interests and achievements in this area.

Outcomes and review

In the way that we expect to critically review our own teaching and research, there needs to be a transparent review of reward processes in relation to teaching, not simply to track the effectiveness of processes but also to ensure that academic and professional service staff perceive that teaching achievements are valued. Equality monitoring will already be in place, but it needs to be extended to include differing career routes. This means looking at the proportions of staff promoted in each grade up to and including full professor. It might also mean looking at the length of time it takes to be promoted at a particular grade.

With these processes in place – supporting the building of education-focused careers within an institution, developing an agreed vocabulary of what constitutes teaching achievement, and transparent and equitable promotion procedures – staff will feel that all career paths are valued by an institution.

Embedding the evidencing of teaching achievements in an institution's culture has a role not only in supporting and rewarding staff, but in achieving institutional goals. This involves applicants and their mentors, but also university senior leadership, line managers and human resources departments. It is only by developing shared understandings across an entire institution of what constitutes teaching achievement and how it is best evidenced that transparent, fair and equitable procedures for recognition and reward can be established.

Critical issues

Internal communications

For universities hoping to achieve parity of esteem for the teaching and learning promotion pathway with that for research, wide-reaching communications work may be needed. Research has shown that academics are slow to trust learning and teaching pathways to promotion (Cashmore and Ramsden, 2009a, 2009b). This can even be true when colleagues in the same school or department have already achieved it (Grimwood and McHanwell, 2013).

Fair and equitable promotion systems depend on promotion criteria being accurately and consistently interpreted across the institution. Yet this is not straightforward. What the criteria mean is as much about how they are implemented in practice as what they say on paper, and this varies between contexts, as well as presenting consistency challenges across disciplines. Terms like 'high quality', 'sustained' and 'significant' require value judgements on the part of applicants and reviewers. In the case of learning and teaching promotions, a shared understanding of what constitutes achievement impact at a particular job grade may not be well established. This is one reason why promotion criteria which have been carefully presented on paper may not deliver the expected results. There is much universities can do to mitigate this risk (as this chapter explores) but it is arguably impossible to avoid it entirely: the varied nature of academic disciplines, the divergent career pathways possible within them and the ways in which achievements may be combined over a set period of years mean that each application needs to be evaluated on its own terms. For this reason, criteria should avoid being over-prescriptive about achievements and focus on broader questions of scope of impact and sphere of influence (see Chapter 4).

The main implication of this is the need for strong communications. There needs to be a consistent understanding of the criteria, and the nature and limits of their flexibility, across all those involved in promotion: decision-makers, human resources colleagues and those involved in staff development. It also includes the applicants themselves, as well as heads of department and others who write references or endorsements for them.

Critical questions for practice

Support strategies

» What opportunities are available for potential applicants to develop their understanding of the promotion criteria, in relation to their own achievements and contributions?

» When were institutional policies and procedures in relation to reward and recognition of teaching last reviewed in your institution? Who was involved, and was there representation from under-represented groups, such as through anonymised focus group data or an EDI committee?

» Do the promotion criteria reflect fully the diversity of education-focused careers?

» Do the process and criteria succeed in recognising the educational, and educational leadership, achievements that are most valued by your institution?

» What opportunities do fully or partially teaching-focused staff have to feed back their experience of pathways and barriers to promotion? How does learning from this feed into changes to process and/or support?

» Are promotion statistics reviewed annually to consider the balance between promotions for teaching and for research?

» Are teaching achievements celebrated in publicity and on websites with equal prominence to those given to research?

Summary

- For reward and recognition processes to be successful, institutions need to have in place policies and processes that fully recognise the diversity of education-focused careers in higher education.

- Parity of esteem in reward and recognition between education and other functions of an institution will be seen in recruitment, retention and motivation of staff and through the formal and informal leadership roles staff will undertake.

- Ensuring a transparent career structure for education-focused staff that is underpinned by a well-conceived support and mentoring scheme is important in ensuring teaching achievements are fully recognised and rewarded.

- Establishing a shared vocabulary for understanding of and evidencing teaching is a vital aspect underpinning full recognition of the value of teaching to an institution.

Useful texts

Advance HE (2013a) *Good Practice Benchmarks*. [online] Available at: www.advance-he.ac.uk/knowledge-hub/promoting-teaching-good-practice-benchmarks (accessed 20 June 2024).

Advance HE (2013b) *Benchmarking Guide*. [online] Available at: www.advance-he.ac.uk/knowledge-hub/promoting-teaching-benchmarking-guide (accessed 20 June 2024).

Two reports describing structured approaches to reviewing promotion procedures.

Graham, R (2015) *Does Teaching Advance Your Academic Career? Interim Report on the Development of a Template for Evaluating Teaching Achievement*. [online] Available at: www.teachingframework.com/resources/Does-teaching-advance-your-academic-career-RAEng-online-report-(April-2015).pdf (accessed 26 July 2024).

Graham, R (2018) *The Career Framework for University Teaching: Background and Overview*. [online] Available at: www.teachingframework.com/resources/Career-Framework-University-Teaching-April-2018.pdf (accessed 2 August 2024).

These two reports describe projects initiated for the Royal Academy of Engineering but are of interest to the wider sector. This project has recently widened, acquiring an international dimension with the Advancing Teaching Initiative (2024).

McHanwell, S and Robson, S (2018) *Guiding Principles for Teaching Promotions*. [online] Available at: www.advance-he.ac.uk/knowledge-hub/guiding-principles-teaching-promotions (accessed 20 June 2024).

The purpose of this report was to review the recommendations of the Promoting Teaching project in light of the multiple perspectives on reward and recognition for teaching excellence reflected in subsequent HEA projects and literature in the field. It proposes a set of guiding principles for the reward and recognition of teaching to inform institutions who may wish to revise their reward and recognition structures to include a clearer focus on teaching.

References

Academy of Medical Sciences (2014) *Redressing the Balance: The Status and Valuation of Teaching in Academic Careers in the Biomedical Sciences*. [online] Available at: https://acmedsci.ac.uk/file-download/35943-53b159424f36e.pdf (accessed 4 August 2024).

Advance HE (2013a) *Good Practice Benchmarks*. [online] Available at: www.advance-he.ac.uk/knowledge-hub/promoting-teaching-good-practice-benchmarks (accessed 20 June 2024).

Advance HE (2013b) *Benchmarking Guide*. [online] Available at: www.advance-he.ac.uk/knowledge-hub/promoting-teaching-benchmarking-guide (accessed 20 June 2024).

Advance HE (2013c) *Making Evidence Count*. [online] Available at: www.advance-he.ac.uk/knowledge-hub/promoting-teaching-making-evidence-count (accessed 20 June 2024).

Advance HE UK (2023a) Professional Standards Framework. [online] Available at: www.advance-he.ac.uk/teaching-and-learning/psf (accessed 20 June 2024).

Advance HE (2023b) NTFS Nominations Resources 2024. [online] Available at: www.advance-he.ac.uk/knowledge-hub/NTFS/Nominations-Resources (accessed 20 June 2024).

Advance HE (2024) Collaborative Awards for Teaching Excellence (CATE) Scheme. [online] Available at: www.advance-he.ac.uk/awards/teaching-excellence-awards/collaborative-award-for-teaching-excellence (accessed 24 April 2024).

Advancing Teaching (2024) Advancing Teaching. [online] Available at: www.advancingteaching.com (accessed 29 April 2024).

Allen, L, O'Connor, A and Kiermer, V (2019) How Can We Ensure Visibility and Diversity in Research Contributions? How the Contributor Role Taxonomy (Credit) Is Helping the Shift from Authorship to Contributor Ship. *Learned Publishing*, 32: 71–4.

Ashwin, P (2020) Teaching Excellence: Principles for Developing Effective System-Wide Approaches. In Callender, C, Locke, W and Marginson, S (eds) *Changing Higher Education for a Changing World* (pp 131–43). London: Bloomsbury Academic.

Ashwin, P (2021) Developing System-Wide Approaches to Teaching Excellence. *International Higher Education/International Issues*, 105: 9–10.

Atkinson, T and Claxton, G (eds) (2000) *The Intuitive Practitioner: On the Value of Not Always Knowing What One Is Doing*. Maidenhead: Open University Press, McGraw-Hill Education.

Austen, L Donnelly, A, McCaig, C and O'Leary, C (2018) *Evaluation of the National Teaching Fellowship Scheme*. [online] Available at: www.officeforstudents.org.uk/media/914c7e2b-0879-4531-a2c5-585b7d8b2d3a/ofs2018_ntfseval.pdf (accessed 24 April 2024).

Australian Awards for University Teaching (2021) [online] Available at: www.universitiesaustralia.edu.au/policy-submissions/teaching-learning-funding/australian-awards-for-university-teaching (accessed 20 June 2024).

Bamber, V (ed) (2013) Evidencing the Value of Educational Development. *SEDA Special 34*. London: SEDA.

Bamber, R (2020) Our Days Are Numbered: Metrics, Managerialism and Academic Development. *SEDA Paper 125*. London: Staff and Educational Development Association Ltd.

Bamber, V and Stefani, L (2016) Taking Up the Challenge of Evidencing Value in Educational Development: From Theory to Practice. *International Journal for Academic Development*, 21(3): 242–54.

Baumfield, V, Hall, E and Wall, K (2012) *Action Research in Education: Learning through Practitioner Enquiry*. 2nd ed. London: SAGE Publications.

Becher, T and Trowler, P (2001) *Academic Tribes and Territories: Intellectual Enquiry and the Cultures of Disciplines*. 2nd ed. Buckingham: Open University Press.

Berg, M and Seeber, B K (2016) *The Slow Professor*. Toronto: University of Toronto Press.

REFERENCES

Bhopal, K (2020) Gender, Ethnicity and Career Progression in UK Higher Education: A Case Study Analysis. *Research Papers in Education*, 35(6): 706–21.

Biggs, J B and Tang, C K-S. (2022) *Teaching for Quality Learning* at University. 5th ed. Maidenhead: Open University Press.

Blackmore, P (2016) *Prestige in Academic Life: Excellence and Exclusion* Abingdon: Routledge.

Bornmann, L (2017) Measuring Impact in Research Evaluations: A Thorough Discussion of Methods for, Effects of and Problems with Impact Measurements. *Higher Education*, 73: 775–87.

Botham, K A (2015) The Perceived Impact on Academics' Teaching Practice of Engaging with a Higher Education Institution's CPD Scheme. *Innovations in Education and Teaching International*, 55(2): 164–75.

Brand, A, Allen, L, Altman, M, Hlava, M and Scott, J (2015) Beyond Authorship: Attribution, Contribution, Collaboration and Credit. *Learned Publishing*, 28(2): 151–5.

Brennan, J and Williams, R (2004) *Collecting and Using Student Feedback – a Guide to Good Practice*. [online] Available at: www.advance-he.ac.uk/knowledge-hub/collecting-and-using-student-feedback-guide-good-practice (accessed 20 June 2024).

Brink, C (2018) *The Soul of a University*. Bristol: Bristol University Press.

Brookfield, S D (2017) *Becoming a Critically Reflective Teacher*. 2nd ed. San Francisco, CA: Jossey-Bass.

Cashmore, A M and Ramsden, P (2009a) *Reward and Recognition of Teaching in Higher Education: A Collaborative Investigation*. Interim report. The Higher Education Academy and GENIE Centre for Excellence in Teaching and Learning, University of Leicester. York: Higher Education Academy. [online] Available at: www.advance-he.ac.uk/knowledge-hub/reward-and-recognition-teaching-higher-education-collaborative-investigation-interim (accessed 20 June 2024).

Cashmore, A M and Ramsden, P (2009b) *Reward and Recognition of Teaching in Higher Education: Institutional Policies and Their Implementation*. York: Higher Education Academy. [online] Available at: www.advance-he.ac.uk/knowledge-hub/reward-and-recognition-teaching-higher-education-institutional-policies-and-their (accessed 20 June 2024).

Cashmore, A, Cane, C and Cane, R (2013) Rebalancing Promotion in the HE Sector: Is Teaching Excellence Being Rewarded? [online] Available at: www.advance-he.ac.uk/knowledge-hub/rebalancing-promotion-he-sector-teaching-excellence-being-rewarded (accessed 20 June 2024).

Centre for Global Higher Education (2023) The Future Higher Education Workforce in Locally and Globally Engaged HEIs. [online] Available at: www.researchcghe.org/research/the-future-higher-education-workforce-in-locally-and-globally-engaged-heis/ (accessed 30 June 2024).

Chalmers, D (2021) Building Your Career through Teaching. In Hunt, L and Chalmers, D (eds) *University Teaching in Focus: A Learning-Centred Approach* (pp 328–43). 2nd ed. Abingdon: Routledge.

Chan, C K Y and Chen, S W (2023) Conceptualisation of Teaching Excellence: An Analysis of Teaching Excellence Schemes. *Assessment & Evaluation in Higher Education*, 49(4): 485–98.

Chickering, A W and Gamson, Z F (1987) *Seven Principles of Good Practice in Undergraduate Education*. [online] Available at: www.researchgate.net/publication/228044220_Seven_Principles_of_Good_Practice_in_Undergraduate_Education (accessed 15 March 2024).

Chickering, A W and Gamson, Z F (1991) Applying the Seven Principles for Good Practice in Undergraduate Education. *New Directions for Teaching and Learning*, Number 47. San Francisco, CA: Jossey-Bass.

Cleaver, E, Lintern, M and McLinden, M (2014) *Teaching and Learning in Higher Education: Disciplinary Approaches to Educational Enquiry*. London: SAGE Publications.

Coe, R, Aloisi, C, Higgins, S and Major, L E (2014) *What Makes Great Teaching? Review of the Underpinning Research*. [online] Available at: www.suttontrust.com/wp-content/uploads/2014/10/What-Makes-Great-Teaching-REPORT.pdf (accessed 15 March 2024).

Cook-Sather, A, Bahti, M and Ntem, A (2019) *Pedagogical Partnerships*. Elon, NC: Elon University Centre for Engaged Learning.

Cotton, D R E, Miller, W and Kneale, P (2018) The Cinderella of Academia: Is Higher Education Pedagogic Research Undervalued in UK Research Assessment? *Studies in Higher Education*, 43(9): 1625–36.

Daskalopoulou, A (2024) Understanding the Impact of Biased Student Evaluations: An Intersectional Analysis of Academics' Experiences in the UK Higher Education Context. *Studies in Higher Education*. https://doi.org/10.1080/03075079.2024.2306364

Dearing Report (National Committee of Inquiry into Higher Education) (1997) *Higher Education in the Learning Society: Main Report*. London: Her Majesty's Stationery Office.

Debowski, S (2012) *The New Academic: A Strategic Handbook*. Maidenhead: Open University Press.

Edinburgh University Students' Association (2016) *What Does Good Teaching Look Like to Students? An Analysis of Teaching Awards Nomination Data*. [online] Available at: https://issuu.com/eusa/docs/teaching_awards_report_2015_16_issu (accessed 22 April 2024).

Exley, K and Dennick, R (2009) *Giving A Lecture: From Presenting to Teaching*. 2nd ed. London: Routledge.

Fan, Y, Shepherd, L J, Slavich, E, Waters, D, Stone, M, Abel, R and Johnston, E (2019) Gender and Cultural Bias in Student Evaluations: Why Representation Matters. *PLoS One*, 14(2): e0209749.

Fanghanel, J (2012) *Being an Academic*. London: Routledge.

Fanghanel, J, Pritchard, J, Potter, J and Wisker, G (2016) *Defining and Supporting the Scholarship of Teaching and Learning (SoTL): A Sector-Wide Study*. [online] Available at: www.advance-he.ac.uk/knowledge-hub/defining-and-supporting-scholarship-teaching-and-learning-sotl-sector-wide-study (accessed 20 June 2024).

Fitzpatrick, M and Moore, S (2015) Exploring Both Positive and Negative Experiences Associated with Engaging in Teaching Awards in a Higher Education Context. *Innovations in Education and Teaching International*, 52(6): 621–31.

French, A and O'Leary, M (eds) (2017) *Teaching Excellence in Higher Education: Challenges, Changes and the Teaching Excellence Framework*. Bingley: Emerald Publications Ltd.

Fung, D and Gordon, C (2016) *Rewarding Educators and Education Leaders in Research-Intensive Universities*. [online] Available at: www.advance-he.ac.uk/knowledge-hub/rewarding-educators-and-education-leaders (accessed 20 June 2024).

Gibbs, G (2010) *Dimensions of Quality*. York: Higher Education Academy.

Gibbs, G (2012) *Implications of 'Dimensions of Quality' in a Market Environment*. York: Higher Education Academy.

Gibbs, G (2016) Teaching. In Higher Education Policy Institute, *Response to the Higher Education Green Paper* (pp 11–26). HEPI report 81. [online] Available at: www.hepi.ac.uk/wp-content/uploads/2016/01/STRICTLY-EMBARGOED-UNTIL-7-JANUARY-2016-FINAL-GREEN-PAPER-RESPONSE-21_12_15-Screen.pdf (accessed 22 April 2024).

Gourlay, L and Stephenson J (2017) Teaching Excellence in Higher Education: Critical Perspectives. *Teaching in Higher Education*, 22(4): 391–5.

Greatbatch, D and Holland, J (2016) *Teaching Quality in Higher Education: Literature Review and Qualitative Research*. [online] Available at: www.researchgate.net/publication/312024245_Teaching_Quality_in_Higher_Education_Literature_Review_and_Qualitative_Research (accessed 15 March 2024).

Grimwood, M and McHanwell, S (2013) Rewarding and Recognising Teaching at a Research-Intensive University. *Educational Developments*, 14: 2. [online] Available at: www.seda.ac.uk/wp-content/uploads/2020/09/Educational-Developments-14.pdf (accessed 4 July 2024).

Gunn, A (2023) *Teaching Excellence? Universities in an Age of Student Consumerism*. Thousand Oaks, CA: SAGE Publications.

Gunn, V and Fisk, A (2013) *Considering Teaching Excellence in Higher Education: 2007–2013. A Literature Review since the CHERI Report 2007*. [online] Available at: www.advance-he.ac.uk/knowledge-hub/considering-teaching-excellence-higher-education-2007-2013 (accessed 15 March 2024).

Harvey, M, Ambler, T and Cahir, J (2017) Spectrum Approach to Mentoring: An Evidence-Based Approach to Mentoring for Academics Working in Higher Education. *Teacher Development*, 21(1): 160–74.

Healey, M, Matthews, K E and Cook-Sather, A (2020) *Writing about Learning and Teaching in Higher Education: Creating and Contributing to Scholarly Conversations Across a Range of Genres*. Elon, NC: Elon

University. [online] Available at: www.centerforengagedlearning.org/books/writing-about-learning (accessed 15 March 2024).

Hillman, N and Harris, J (2019) *Recognising Teachers in the Life Sciences*. [online] Available at: https://static.physoc.org/app/uploads/2019/04/22192917/Recognising-Teachers-in-the-Life-Sciences.pdf (accessed 5 August 2024).

Hoorens, V, Dekker, G and Deschrijver, E (2021) Gender Bias in Student Evaluations of Teaching: Students' Self-Affirmation Reduces the Bias by Lowering Evaluations of Male Professors. *Sex Roles*, 84(1–2): 34–48.

Husbands, C and Pearce J (2012) *What Makes Great Pedagogy? Nine Claims from Research*. [online] Available at: https://assets.publishing.service.gov.uk/media/5a7e413c40f0b6230268a2a3/what-makes-great-pedagogy-nine-claims-from-research.pdf (accessed 15 March 2024).

Index of Revisions to the 'Guidance on Submissions' 2019/01 REF 2021 (2020) [online] Available at: https://2021.ref.ac.uk/guidance-and-criteria-on-submissions/guidance/index.html (accessed 30 June 2024).

Jarvis, J and Clark, K (2020) *Conversations to Change Teaching*. St Albans: Critical Publishing Ltd.

Ka Yuk Chan, C and Chen, S W (2023) Conceptualisation of Teaching Excellence: An Analysis of Teaching Excellence Schemes. *Assessment & Evaluation in Higher Education*, 49(4): 485–98. https://doi.org/10.1080/02602938.2023.2271188

Kandiko Howson, C and Buckley, A (2020) Quantifying Learning: Measuring Student Outcomes in Higher Education in England. *Politics and Governance*, 8(2): 6–14.

Kara, S and Barton, J (2023) *The Education Awards: TEAs Report 2023*. Newcastle University. [online] Available at: https://fa1748085c52ad15761d-181c25b91e106f7ce7e1130b987dab86.ssl.cf3.rackcdn.com/05029E42_TEAs_Report_2023.pdf (accessed 22 April 2024).

King, H (ed) (2022) *Developing Expertise for Teaching in Higher Education: Practical Ideas for Professional Learning and Development*. Abingdon: Routledge.

Kneebone, R (2022) Foreword. In King, H (ed) *Developing Expertise for Teaching in Higher Education: Practical Ideas for Professional Learning and Development*. Abingdon: Routledge.

Knight, R-A (2021) *Supporting Individuals to Apply for Reward and Recognition – The DRIVE Model of Evidencing Educational Impact*. [online] Available at: https://blogs.city.ac.uk/learningatcity/2021/03/18/supporting-individuals-to-apply-for-reward-and-recognition-the-drive-model-of-evidencing-educational-impact/ (accessed 30 June 2024).

Kreber, C (2013) *Authenticity in and through Teaching in Higher Education: The Transformative Potential of the Scholarship of Teaching*. Abingdon: Routledge.

Lea, J (ed) (2015) *Enhancing Learning and Teaching in Higher Education: Engaging with the Dimensions of Practice*. Maidenhead: McGraw Hill Education, Open University Press.

Levander, S, Forsberg, E and Elmgren, M (2020) The Meaning-Making of Educational Proficiency in Academic Hiring: A Blind Spot in the Black Box. *Teaching in Higher Education*, 25(5): 541–59.

Light, G, Cox, R and Calkins, S (2009) *Learning and Teaching in Higher Education: The Reflective Professional*. 2nd ed. London: SAGE Publications.

Locke, W (2014) *Shifting Academic Careers: Implications for Enhancing Professionalism in Teaching and Supporting Learning*. [online] Available at: www.advance-he.ac.uk/knowledge-hub/shifting-academic-careers-implications-enhancing-professionalism-teaching-and (accessed 20 June 2024).

Locke, W (2016) *Shifting Landscapes: Meeting the Staff Development Needs of the Changing Academic Workforce*. [online] Available at: www.advance-he.ac.uk/knowledge-hub/shifting-landscapes (accessed 20 June 2024).

Lubicz-Nawrocka, T and Bunting, K (2019) Student Perceptions of Teaching Excellence: An Analysis of Student-Led Teaching Award Nomination Data. *Teaching in Higher Education*, 24(1): 63–80.

Macfarlane, B (2007) Beyond Performance in Teaching Excellence. In Skelton, A E (ed) *International Perspectives on Teaching Excellence in Higher Education: Improving Knowledge and Practice* (pp 48–59). Abingdon: Routledge.

Mann, S and Walsh, S (2013) RP or 'Rip': A Critical Perspective on Reflective Practice. *Applied Linguistics Review*, 4(2): 291–315.

Mayer, A, Blair, J, Ko, M, Patel, S and Files, J (2014) Long-Term Follow-Up of a Facilitated Peer Mentoring Program. *Medical Teacher*, 36(3): 260–6.

McHanwell, S and Robson, S (2018) *Guiding Principles for Teaching Promotions*. [online] Available at: www.advance-he.ac.uk/knowledge-hub/guiding-principles-teaching-promotions (accessed 20 June 2024).

Munir, F (2022) Sponsorship Mentoring: Development Resources for Higher Education. Advance HE. [online] Available at: www.advance-he.ac.uk/knowledge-hub/sponsorship-mentoring-development-resources-higher-education-institutions (accessed 19 March 2024).

Murray, R (2015) *Writing in Social Spaces: A Social Processes Approach to Academic Writing*. London; New York: Routledge.

Nixon, J (2007) Excellence and the Good Society. In Skelton, A (ed) *International Perspectives on Teaching Excellence in Higher Education: Improving Knowledge and Practice* (pp 15–31). Abingdon: Routledge.

Noble, H and Heale, R (2019) Triangulation in Research, with Examples. *Evidence Based Nursing*, 22(3): 67–8.

O'Donovan, R (2024) Missing the Forest for the Trees: Investigating Factors Influencing Student Evaluations of Teaching. *Assessment & Evaluation in Higher Education*, 49(4): 453–70.

O'Leary, M (2017) Monitoring and Measuring Teaching Excellence in Higher Education: From Contrived Co-operation to Collective Collaboration. In French, A and O'Leary, M (eds) *Teaching Excellence in Higher Education* (pp 75–107). Bingley: Emerald Publishing Ltd.

Ockene, J, Milner, R, Thorndyke, L, Congdon, J and Cain, J (2017) Peers for Promotion: Achieving Academic Advancement through Facilitated Peer Mentoring. *Journal of Faculty Development*, 31(3): 5–13.

Peat, J (2015) Getting Down to the Nitty-Gritty: The Trials and Tribulations of an Institutional Professional Recognition Scheme. *Perspectives: Policy and Practice in Higher Education*, 19(3): 92–5.

Probert, B (2013) *Teaching-Focussed Appointments in Australian Universities*. [online] Available at: https://ltr.edu.au/resources/Teaching-focused_academic_appointments.pdf. (accessed 20 June 2024).

QS World University Rankings (2023) [online] Available at: https://support.qs.com/hc/en-gb/articles/4405955370898-QS-World-University-Rankings- (accessed 20 June 2024).

Race, P (2001) *The Lecturer's Toolkit*. 2nd ed. London: Kogan Page.

Rickinson, M, Spencer, R and Stainton, C (2012) *NTFS Review: Report on Findings*. [online] Available at: www.advance-he.ac.uk/knowledge-hub/ntfs-review-2012-report-findings (accessed 3 April 2024).

Seppala, N and Smith, C (2019) Teaching Awards in Higher Education: A Qualitative Study of Motivation and Outcomes. *Studies in Higher Education*, 45(7): 1398–412.

Shephard, K, Harland, T, Stein, S and Tidswell, T (2010) Preparing an Application for a Higher-Education Teaching-Excellence Award: Whose Foot Fits Cinderella's Shoe? *Journal of Higher Education Policy and Management*, 33(1): 47–56.

Shepherd, S (2017) Why Are There So Few Female Leaders in Higher Education: A Case of Structure or Agency? *Management in Education*, 31: 2: 81–7.

Shulman, L S (1987) Knowledge and Teaching: Foundations of the New Reforms. *Harvard Educational Review*, 57(1): 1–22.

Skelton, A (2004) Understanding Teaching Excellence in Higher Education: A Critical Evaluation of the National Teaching Fellowships Scheme. *Studies in Higher Education*, 29: 451–68.

Skelton, A (2005) *Understanding Teaching Excellence in Higher Education: Towards a Critical Approach*. Abingdon: Routledge.

Smart, F and Popovic, C (2021) *Educational Developers Thinking Allowed*. [online] Available at: https://edta.info.yorku.ca (accessed 11 March 2024).

Smart, F, Dransfield, M, Floyd, S and Davies, V (2021) Dialogic Assessment in the Context of Professional Recognition: Perspectives from the Canoe. *Journal of Perspectives in Applied Academic Practice*, 9(1): 36–43.

Smith, S and Walker, D (2021) Scholarship and Academic Capitals: The Boundaried Nature of Education-Focused Career Tracks. *Teaching in Higher Education*, 29(1): 111–25.

REFERENCES

Society for Teaching and Learning in Higher Education (2021) 3M National Teaching Fellowship Scheme. [online] Available at: www.stlhe.ca/awards/3m-national-teaching-fellowship (accessed 20 June 2024).

Spowart, L and Turner, R (2020) Assessing the Impact of Accreditation on Institutions: Literature Review. [online] Available at: https://advance-he.ac.uk/knowledge-hub/assessing-impact-accreditation-institutions (accessed 15 March 2024).

Swartzel, K (2021) University Unwritten Rules for a Successful Academic Career. *Academia Letters*, article 572. [online] Available at: https://doi.org/10.20935/AL572 (accessed 22 March 2024).

The World Cafe (2022) The World Cafe Method. [online] Available at: www.theworldcafe.com/key-concepts-resources/world-cafe-method (accessed 20 June 2024).

Thompson, S and Zaitseva, E (2012) *Reward and Recognition: Student Led Teaching Awards Report*. [online] Available at: https://s3.eu-west-2.amazonaws.com/assets.creode.advancehe-document-manager/documents/hea/private/resources/reward-recognition-slta-report_1568037060.pdf (accessed 22 April 2024).

Tomlinson, M, Enders, J and Naidoo, R (2020) The Teaching Excellence Framework: Symbolic Violence and the Measured Market in Higher Education. *Critical Studies in Education*, 61(5): 627–42.

Wakeling, L, Jakubovics, N, McHanwell, S and Stewart, J (2016) Challenging the Basic Sciences 'Learn and Forget' Culture. *Medical Education*, 50: 578–9.

Weller, S (2019) *Academic Practice: Developing as a Professional in Higher Education*. 2nd ed. London: SAGE Publications.

Whitchurch, C (2023) The Changing Profile and Work Experiences of Higher Education Staff in the 21st Century. [online] Available at: www.hepi.ac.uk/2023/08/18/the-changing-profile-and-work-experiences-of-higher-education-staff-in-the-21st-century (accessed 18 March 2024).

Whitchurch, C, Locke, W and Giulio Marini, G (2023) *Challenging Approaches to Academic Career-Making*. London: Bloomsbury Publishing.

Wood, M and Su, F (2017) What Makes an Excellent Lecturer? Academic's Perceptions on the Discourse of 'Teaching Excellence' in Higher Education. *Teaching in Higher Education*, 22(4): 451–66.

Wren Butler, J (2021) Legibility Zones: An Empirically-Informed Framework for Considering Unbelonging and Exclusion in Contemporary English Academia. *Social Inclusion*, 9(3): 16–26.

Wyse, D, Brown, C, Oliver, S and Poblete, X (2018) *The BERA Close-to-Practice Research Project: Research Report*. London: British Educational Research Association. [online] Available at: www.bera.ac.uk/researchers-resources/publications/bera-statement-on-close-topractice-research (accessed 30 June 2024).

Zambrana, R E, Ray, R, Espino, M M, Castro, C, Cohen, B D and Eliason, J (2015) 'Don't Leave Us Behind': The Importance of Mentoring for Underrepresented Minority Faculty. *American Educational Research Journal*, 52(1): 40–72.

Index

360-degree feedback, 54
3M scheme (Canada), 62

Academic Ranking of World Universities (ARWU), 4
academic reputation, 5
academic workforce, 89
Advance HE, 16, 40, 45, 51, 61, 63
Advancing Teaching, The, project, 51
annual appraisal, 69, 74
application, developing, 68–9. *See also* institutional support for awards/promotion applicants
    drafting, 70, 71–2
    pre-writing and planning, 70–1
    time commitment, 84–5
Association for Learning Technology (ALT), 61
awards. *See* teaching awards

Beckingham, Sue, 32
Blackstone, Tessa, 10
British Educational Research Association (BERA), 34

Career Framework for University Teaching, 51
close-to-practice research, 46, 90
CMALT Accreditation Framework, 61
Collaborative Award for Teaching Excellence (CATE), 63, 84
Collecting and Using Student Feedback, 48
confidentiality, 2, 95
continuing professional development (CPD), 13, 15, 27–30, 61, 62
contributions to profession (teaching award criteria), 15
curriculum
    development, 45–6
    innovation, 69
    review, 41, 44, 53

discipline mastery, 12
dissemination of practice, 33–6
DRIVE model, 67
Drumm, Louise, 33

Edinburgh University Students' Association, 14
educational enquiry
    collaboration with colleagues, 34
    contribution to, 34
    dissemination of, 33–6
    scholarship of teaching and learning (SoTL), 35–6
    starting point for, 34–5
educational journals, 34
education-focused career, 25
    contribution to leadership, 26
    dissemination of practice and educational research/enquiry, 33–6
    diversity in, 90–1
    evolving landscape/opportunities of higher education, 38
    identification of myths about, 25–6
    individual practice in teaching and/or learning support, 30
    issues to consider, 37–8
    leading and co-ordinating practice, 30–3
    professional learning and development, 27–30
    promotion of teaching, 26
    structures and pathways, 37–8
    teaching as a career dead end, 26
esteem indicators, 51
evidence-informed/evidence-led teaching, 22
expertise
    developing, 30
    in teaching, 20
    subject, 12
external engagement, 30, 33, 37
external fellowships, 42
external recognition, evidence from, 51

feedback, 15, 55, 86
    peer, 44–5
    student, 13, 44, 49, 69
    360-degree, 54
focus groups, 44, 49
free text comments, 43, 44, 49

'going the extra mile', 11, 14, 15, 16
good teaching, 12. *See also* teaching excellence
  research attempts to define, 11–12
  student feedback on, 13
  themes of, 12–13
graduate earnings, 43
group discussions, 49
Guardian, The, 4

Hejmadi, Momna, 20–1
Higher Education Academy (HEA), 14, 41, 89, 91–2
Humboldt model of higher education, 89

identity and career progression aspects, conflict between, 83–4
impact of teaching activity, 16, 54, 55, 63, 66, 68, 84
imposter syndrome, 74
informal discussions, 70, 81
institutional perspectives on teaching evidence, 88
  benefits for institutions, 89–90
  institutional considerations in supporting applicants, 95–7
  internal communications, 97–8
  outcomes and review, 97
  policies and procedures, 90–3
  Promoting Teaching Project, 91–2
  value of support/mentoring to staff and institutions, 94–7
institutional support for awards/promotion applicants, 74–5
  blending individual and group support, 76–7
  boundaries and limitations of, 75
  career progression aspects and values/identity, conflict between, 83–4
  difficulties with writing, 81–3
  encouraging participants to take up support, 77
  experience of staff, 75
  focus of, 78–9
  minorities, 76
  setting up, 75–6
  showing individual impact in collaborative achievement, 84
  structural inequities, 78
  structuring support, 79–81
  struggle with time commitment, 84–5
  timing of support, 75
  unsuccessful applications, 85–6
institutional teaching award schemes, 50, 62
internal communications, 97–8
international SoTL (ISoTL), 46

Journal of Multidisciplinary Graduate Research, The, 36

King, Nicola, 60–1

leadership, 20, 25, 42, 46, 47, 51, 54, 63, 68, 89–90
  contribution to, 26
  and promotion, 60
  roles, 30–3
learning gain, 43

Making Evidence Count, 45, 46, 51
marketisation of higher education, 2, 7
mentors/mentoring, 37, 50, 60, 74, 88, 90, 93. *See also* institutional support for awards/promotion applicants
  experience of staff, 75
  spectrum approach to, 76
  sponsorship, 78
  value to staff and institutions, 94–7
methods of instruction, competence in, 12
missions of universities, variation in, 3, 17–18
mixed methods approach, 2, 40, 42

narrative, 42, 48, 49, 55, 58, 63, 65
  activity, 65
  centrepiece of, 68
  DRIVE model, 67
  of impact, 66, 80
  motivating factors, 66
  story-telling and box-ticking, 67–8
National Student Survey (NSS), 6
national teaching awards, 62
National Teaching Fellowship Scheme (NTFS), 15–16, 41, 64
networking, 30, 34, 37
Newcastle University, 14, 76–7

online learning, 13, 31, 33
online resources, publishing, 55
online surveys, 49

parity of esteem, 2, 6–7, 8, 10, 17, 19, 64, 89, 90, 94, 95, 96, 97
pedagogical content knowledge, significance of, 12
pedagogical scholarship. *See* scholarship of teaching and learning (SoTL)
peer review, 7, 44, 48, 50, 95
peer(s)
  evidence from, 50, 51, 54
  external recognition from, 51
  feedback, 44–5
  mentoring, 76
  observation of teaching, 50
peer-reviewed journals, 36
personal practice (teaching award criteria), 14–15
Practice and Evidence of the Scholarship of Teaching and Learning in Higher Education (PESTLHE), 36
Practice: Contemporary Issues in Professional Learning, 36
Principal Fellowship of the Higher Education Academy (PFHEA), 51
professional learning and development, 12, 15, 16, 27, 41, 45, 46
  critical approach to, 28–30
  engaging in, 27
  reflecting on, 28
professional recognition, 61–2. *See also* reward and recognition
Professional Standards Framework (PSF), 40, 41, 42, 58, 61
Professional Statutory and Regulatory Bodies (PSRBs), 18
Promoting Teaching Project, 91–2
promotion, 31–2, 41, 42, 69. *See also* institutional perspectives on teaching evidence; institutional support for awards/promotion applicants; writing
  application, writing, 58–60
  briefings, 70
  criteria for, 11, 58–9, 69–70, 79, 81, 83, 90, 93, 98
  disparities, between teaching and research, 17
  supporting statements, 95
  and working in teams, 53
proportion of good degrees measure, 6

QS World University Rankings, 4, 5
quality in higher education, 3–6
questionnaires, 13, 44, 48, 49

ranking tables. *See* university ranking tables
ratios of staff to students measure, 6
reach of teaching activity, 16, 63
reflective practice, 15, 22
reflective writing, 82–3
research, 18, 46, 89
  career, pathways of, 26
  close-to-practice, 46, 90
  excellence, 3, 17, 68
  as a measure of university prestige, 7, 10
  performance, over-emphasis in university ranking tables, 5
  privileging of, 74
  reputation, and academic reputation, 5
  and teaching, parity of esteem between, 2, 6–7, 10, 17, 95
research and education contracts, staff with, 7
Research Excellence Framework (REF), 18, 35
research-based teaching, 6
research-led teaching, 6
reward and recognition, 2, 19, 41, 43, 44, 74, 75, 78, 88, 94. *See also* institutional perspectives on teaching evidence; writing
  barriers to rewarding teaching excellence, 94
  benefits for institutions, 89–90
  evidence from external recognition, 51
  and teaching excellence, 17
Rose, David, 47–8
Royal Academy of Engineering, 51

scholarship, 34, 46, 61
scholarship of teaching and learning (SoTL), 1, 34, 35–6, 46, 90
scope of activity, 45–6, 47, 59
self-reflection, 41
Society for Research in Higher Education (SRHE), 34
Society for Teaching and Learning in Higher Education (STLHE), 62
spectrum approach to mentoring, 76
sphere of influence, 46–7, 55, 59
sponsorship mentoring, 78

Staff and Educational Development
    Association (SEDA) Fellowships
    Scheme, 61
structural inequities, 78
student assessment outcomes, 43, 44
student engagement, 45, 48
student evaluation
    quantitative data, 48-9
    questionnaires, 13, 44, 48
    scores for staff, 43
student satisfaction, 5, 33, 61
student–teacher interactions, quality of, 12
Sunday Times, The, 4
supporting statements, 95
surveys, 5, 13, 44, 48, 49, 69

teacher excellence, 13-16
teaching awards, 11, 14-15, 45. *See also*
    institutional support for awards/
    promotion applicants; National Teaching
    Fellowship Scheme (NTFS); writing
    application, 42, 62-5
    criteria, 14-15, 79
    institutional, 50, 62
    national, 51, 62
    schemes, value of, 63-5
    student-led, 13, 14, 48, 62
    working in teams, 53, 63
teaching effectiveness, evidence for, 1, 40, 88.
    See also writing
    access to, 42
    adapting to specific purposes, 42
    criticality and exploration by teachers, 1
    difficulties in, 2
    diverse nature of higher education
        teaching, 42
    evidence from external recognition, 51
    evidence from peers, 50, 51, 54
    evidence from students, 48-9
    evidence gathering when working in
        teams, 53-4
    gathering, 52
    impact of teaching, 55
    importance of, 7-8
    marketisation of higher education, 2, 7
    nature of teaching evidence, 43-5
    quality of, 55
    reasons for gathering, 40, 41-2
    scope of activity, 45-6, 59

sources of, 48-51, 59
sphere of influence, 46-7, 59
tensions between research and
    teaching, 2, 6-7
time of evidence gathering, 54
teaching excellence, 1, 2, 3, 10, 16-18, 64, 74,
    88. *See also* awards, teaching
    barriers to rewarding, 94
    as a contested concept, 11
    DRIVE model, 67
    drivers for demonstrating, 16
    experts and expertise in teaching, 20
    as a goal attainable by few people, 19
    individual teaching performance, 11-13
    literature, discourses in, 10
    measures, 5-6
    measuring, 18-19
    and missions of universities, 17-18
    National Teaching Fellowship
        Scheme, 15-16
    as a neoliberal strategy, 17
    research attempts to define good
        teaching, 11-12
    and reward and recognition, 17
    taxonomy for defining, 11
    themes of good teaching, 12-13
    understanding of student learning,
        12-13
    and university teaching missions, 6
Teaching Excellence Framework (TEF), 18
Teaching in Higher Education, 36
teaching portfolio, 55, 60
teams, working in, 42, 51
    and awards, 63
    gathering evidence about teaching
        effectiveness, 53-4
textbooks, 55
'ticket out of class' approach, 49
Times Higher Education, 4
Times, The, 4
'traffic light' approach, 49

University of Wollongong, 50
university ranking tables, 3-5
    criterion for position of universities/
        subjects in, 5
    and knowledge development, 3
    over-emphasis of research performance, 5
    prestige effects, 3

sample, 4
variation in missions of universities, 3, 17–18

value of teaching activity, 16, 63, 67–8
values, 66, 68
   conflict with career progression aspects, 83–4
   -led approach to learning, 47

word limits of application, 68
writing, 58, 96
   developing an application, 68–72
   difficulties with, 81–3
   narrative, 65–7
   promotion application, 58–60
   reflective, 82–3
   teaching awards application, 62–5